MYNOR SCHULT

Machu Picchu & Amazon River

Praise About the Book

"Charming testimony and a guide to the transformative power of nature available to all and worthy of being cared for by all." Viviana Fernandez; Anchor/Producer at CNN EN ESPAÑOL

Fantastic, fantastic, fantastic!!! What else would I say... thanks for such great and accurate information. What a great Amazon book. Denis Vazquez, Panama   Reporter for DoVa News, Panama

I previewed "Amazon River" and find the book as an excellent guide not only to explore the river for the first time, but as an excellent reference for anyone interested in learning more about the Amazon. The topic is very relevant and appropriate in these times of global warming. Dra. Donna Schwontkowski, (Poland) M.S. in Nutrition & Master Herbalist author of the book "Traditional Herbs From the Amazon" TV Presenter.

"Every little bit of rain forest that gets ripped out over there... really hurts us over here." **Harrison Ford (USA) Movie star of Indiana Jones and Air Force One**

ESPECTACULAR! CONGRATULATIONS! Today, I managed to read more than 40 pages of this very readable and informative book. It has aroused my interest to go back to the Amazon, and I will use this book for my future journey from Coca to Belem." *Mario Cifuentes, (Colombia) Owner of Hotel Hacienda El Eden, Cali, Colombia*

"I want to thank you for making my Amazon trip so easy. I saved hundreds of pounds that allowed me to see so much more of the river. THANK YOU!!! Jennifer Glazer (England)

Everything was perfect!!!! Everything went WONDERFUL!!! The Amazon was amazingly beautiful just like your book describes it. I enjoyed the early exercise and your coaching sessions were enlightening. Perfect sunsets with a great coach. Karen O'Donnel, (Australia) CEO Australian Adventures

AmazonRiverExpert.com

"Each of us must take a greater personal responsibility for this deteriorating global environment"

Al Gore,(USA) *Nobel Peace Prize & Vice-President "Earth in the Balance"*

This book is for dreamers. It's the ultimate "one day I will..." type of book. Even if you don't have included the Amazon in your Bucket List, after reading this book, you probably will. *Edna Olivera, Psicologist Universidad Catolica, Colombia*

For the latest testimonials on books, tours and other products from Mynor Schult and the Amazon rainforest visit
www.AmazonRiverExpert.com

ALSO BY MYNOR SCHULT

Amazon The River For The First Time... And Forever
How to Travel the river from beginning to end

Amazon River Peru
Traveling safely, economically and ecologically

Amazon River Colombia
Safely navigating remote Amazonian waters

Amazon River Brazil
Traveling safely, economically and ecologically

Life Lessons From the Amazon
Ancient coaching principles to create the best year of your life (every year!)

Machu Picchu

&

Amazon River

Traveling Safely, Economically and Ecologically

MYNOR SCHULT

Amazon
RIVEREXPERT.COM

MYNOR SCHULT

Copyright © 2011 by MYNOR SCHULT

All rights reserved, including the right to reproduce this book or portions thereof in any form whatsoever. For information address Amazon River Expert Rights Department, Murrieta, CA, USA.

ISBN-13:
978-1466467071
ISBN-10:
146646707X

Library of Congress Cataloging-in-Publication Data is available upon request.

Front Cover Designed by Luis Rafael Bonilla M.

Printed in the United States of America. First Edition.
No part of this book may be used or reproduced in any manner whatsoever without written permission except in the case of brief quotations embodied in critical articles and reviews; or except as provided by U. S. copyright law. For more information address the author or AmazonRiverExpert.com.

Amazon River books may be purchased for educational, business or sales promotional use. To bring the author to your live event contact AmazonRiverExpert.com (+1 858 222 1077)

Machu Picchu & Amazon River

Copyright Notice

All rights reserved. No part of this publication may be reproduced or transmitted in any form or by any means, including electronic or mechanical. Any unauthorized use, sharing, reproduction, or distribution of parts herein is strictly prohibited. You may NOT distribute this document, edit, or reprint its content.

While attempts have been made to verify the correctness and reliability of the information provided in this publication, the author and publisher do not assume any responsibilities for errors, omissions, or contradictory information contained in this document. The author and publisher are not liable for any losses or damages whatsoever, including, but not limited to, the loss of business, profits, service, clients, information, or any other pecuniary loss. The information contained in this document is not intended as advice (legal, medical, financial or otherwise) and is provided for traveling and educational purposes only. You are highly encouraged to seek the advice of a competent professional when applicable.

The reader of this book assumes all responsibility and liability for the use of these materials and information. Mynor Schult, AmazonRiverExpert.com, and its affiliates assume no responsibility or liability whatsoever on behalf of the reader of these materials.

Any results depicted or implied in this document are atypical of most results. No guarantees, promises, or suggestions of any results are made, whether implied or stated. Individual results may vary from those shown, and everything herein is provided on an "at your own risk" basis.

While the author has done his earnest best to make sure that you enjoy this report, certain grammatical and typographical errors may still exist. Any such error, or any perceived slight of a specific person or organization, is purely unintentional. Wherever the neuter is not used, any one gender was chosen for simplicity's sake. This document was created with the hope that the reader finds its content useful and not analyzed for the purposes of gender equality, language correctness, or writing style. Words, phrases, ads, and graphics, whether followed by "TM," "SM" and "®" or not, are trademarks and servicemarks of AmazonRiverExpert.com or are the trademarks and servicemarks of their respective owners, whether indicated or not.

Please help protect and conserve the environment

Table of Contents

Praise About the Book 3

Copyright Notice 9

Table of Contents 10

SPECIAL DEDICATION 15

About the Author 17

About This Book 19

INTRODUCTION 22

    Why Should You Care? 22

    Is This Book For You? 24

    Take the Challenge 25

    About Your Visa 28

HEADING TO PERU 29

Peru 30

    Lima 32

    Peru's Highways. 32

    Public Transportation 34

    El Metropolitano 35

Machu Picchu & Amazon River

- Lima Metro 35
- Reaching Lima by Air 36

HEADING TO MACHU PICCHU 41

- Arriving Cuzco 42
- Reaching Cuzco By Air 43
- Reaching Cuzco By Bus 44
- Buses to Machu Picchu 45

MACHU PICCHU 48

- The Inca Trail 53
- From the Sacred Valley to Machu Picchu 57
- Practical Information for Trekkers: 63
- Items Need for the Trip 66
- When to go 67
- Preparing for Your Trek 68
- Inca Trail Tour Agencies 72
- Inca Trail Regulations 75
- Day-by-Day: Classic 4-Day Inca Trek 77
- Alternatives to the Inca Trail 82
- Machu Picchu Striking Facts 85

HEADING TO THE AMAZON 91

The Most Beautiful Journey on Earth 92

    Amazon Striking Facts..97

THE BEST JOURNEY OF YOUR LIFE 102

    The Beginning Was Controversial 108

    Sector Divisions 111

    The Amazon Basin is Vast and Expansive 113

    Is Colombia Safe? 115

NAVIGATING REMOTE AMAZON WATERS 118

IQUITOS CITY 122

    Getting To Iquitos...131

    Iquitos By Air:..131

    River Transport...133

    The Apex of 3 South American Countries..............137

FROM MANAUS' JUNGLES TO BELEM'S BEACHES 148

CONSERVATION AND SUSTAINABLE TOURISM 150

    The Responsible Tourist and Traveler 156

INDIGENOUS CULTURES..160

    Are They Like Canaries in a Mine? 169

    Thank You! 170

RESOURCES FOR YOUR AMAZON TRIP..........................171

Machu Picchu & Amazon River

Airports 171

Airlines 172

Buses 173

Boats 173

More Interesting Places 174

Aditional Resources 175

Videos that you must watch 176

Notes 178

MYNOR SCHULT

"Let every individual and institution now think and act as a responsible trustee of Earth, seeking choices in ecology, economics and ethics that will provide a sustainable future, eliminate pollution, poverty and violence, awaken the wonder of life and foster peaceful progress in the human adventure."

— John McConnell,

founder of International Earth Day

SPECIAL DEDICATION

I enthusiastically dedicate this book to a person that did not care a whole lot about this book. As a matter of fact he was a major distraction during my writing sessions, especially at night when trying to sleep for a couple of hours became a true adventure.

To my grandson Cannon who was born just a few days ago. We welcome you to the jungle. Life is fantastic and there are many beautiful places for us to explore. Hurry up and grow fast so that together we can discover the universe.

I love you Cannon Elijah Schult Huffman.

Con todo mi corazón,.. abuelo

"SOS Amazon": every second we lose 1.5 acres of rainforests once covering 14% of earth land surface, now a mere 6%. By WcP.Watchful.Eye

About the Author

After attending his first year at the University of Costa Rica, in the early 80s, Mynor was infected with the beautiful traveler's disease, with results so far incurable. His first big trip started in Nicaragua, a country torn by war. He then crossed the border to El Salvador, another country plagued by guerrilla warfare.

After surviving the crossing of Central America and the Mexican desert, Mynor drove all the way up to Canada before finally settling in USA. Since then, he has accumulated thousands of miles, traveling around the Americas and other continents.

He has worked and lived in Mexico, Colombia, Paraguay, Costa Rica, and many USA cities. Today, his home is in a suitcase, somewhere between Brazil and California. Most recently, Mynor has spent over a year traveling the world, mainly in South America, navigating several rivers in Colombia and Venezuela. It was there that he finally decided to achieve one of his most cherished dreams: to navigate the mighty Amazon River from its inception in Peru to its flows into the beautiful Atlantic coast of Brazil.

After traveling in more than 60 countries, some of

his favorite places are Thailand, Costa Rica, and China; but he lists Colombia and Sweden as countries on the list of places that everyone should visit before they die.

In Costa Rica, his favorite sights include visiting the active Arenal Volcano and lying on the Manuel Antonio beaches.

Currently he is writing "Amazon's Life Lessons", as well as other books on Amazon conservation.

One of his most memorable travel experiences occurred when a herd of monkeys stole his camera and lunch, while Mynor was enjoying the Pacific beaches in Costa Rica.

To learn more about Mynor's travel adventures and find out how you can have some of your own, visit his website: www.AmazonRiverExpert.com

Mynor at the World Sales Forum

About This Book

After I wrote my first bestseller "Amazon the River for the First Time... and Forever" I kept receiving letters from readers wanting to know more about the Inca ruins of Machu Picchu in Peru.

I had considered writing a book solely for that destination, but after few surveys it was obvious that the people that visit the Inca ruins also wanted to visit the Amazon river.

The market investigation also showed that most people visited Machu Picchu even though they really wanted to see the Amazon river. However, fears and concerns of the unknown kept them from visiting the river.

Today I confess that despite many other trips around the world I too had been nervous about visiting both destinations. It was only about 15 years ago that I visited Machu Picchu for the first time. The trip to the Amazon had to wait even longer as I had read too many traveling tales of famous Spanish conquerors, usually with fatal outcomes.

However; in the spring of 2008, I built up my courage and full of fears and questions, I left California, to discover the Amazon river. How safe would this trip be? How long it would take? What resources were necessary to navigate the mighty Amazon from beginning to end?

I am not sure exactly when those fears disappeared, but I remember that it was somewhere between my trip to Machu Picchu and the beginning of my first Amazon trip. Today, with complete certainty, I share that you do not have to be an extreme adventure seeker, like Indiana Jones, to carry out a fascinating journey to any of these destinations.

Thus the idea for this book was born.

With resignation and sadness on behalf of my adventurers' ego, I had to accept that today, thanks to the advances of technology in transportation and communication; these two Peruvian destinations are for everyone. It is for infants and children, traveling with their parents. It is for college students, traveling alone. It is for grandparents, looking for one last adventure.

However, the clock is ticking and before it is too late, due to global warming and deforestation, everyone should visit Machu Picchu and the Amazon to experience the beauty and serenity that unfortunately are rapidly disappearing.

Moreover, the only adventurous spirit required is the same one that you need to visit a national park in the U.S., Australia, Costa Rica or Europe.

Traveling to Machu Picchu or to the origins of the

Machu Picchu & Amazon River

Amazon in Peru is one of the most coveted trips in the life of any traveler, but remember that dreams will never come through unless action is taken to accomplish them.

> *"Twenty years from now you will be more disappointed by the things you didn't do than by the ones you did do. So throw off the bowlines, sail away from the safe harbor. Catch the trade winds in your sails. Explore. Dream. Discover."* – Mark Twain

INTRODUCTION

Congratulations! You are heading to visit worldwide landmarks for our planet. Whether you go first to Machu Picchu or visit the biggest river in the world, you will find people from many cities from around the world.

In addition, I congratulate you in advance because, without a doubt, you will become a better citizen of the world once you are exposed to the mystical ruins of Machu Picchu and the giant Amazon basin. After this fantastic adventure, you will understand more clearly that we are all connected in more than one way and that the oxygen produced here not only benefits all the residents throughout South America, but it also improves the oxygen's quality that you breath in Shanghai, Moscow, Sydney or Mexico City.

Why Should You Care?

Another grand reason to come to remarkable Peru besides being mystified by its sheer beauty, is that it could become a labor of love. No, I am not going to ask you to donate or give away your money, but, without much effort, you could be doing great good for other people. All you need to do are small things, such as buying your souvenirs directly from the locals, especially indigenous people, hiring their services whenever possible and other small things of that nature.

Machu Picchu & Amazon River

The Machu Picchu and Amazon basin are immensely rich places in natural resources and biodiversity. However, few of us know that many people that live there lack some of the most basic financial needs. Therefore, when you visit and practice sustainable and green tourism, you could contribute to make a better world.

During the last few years it has been proven that tourism, when done for the right reasons, helps to eradicate poverty. With sustainable tourism, a good percentage of the profits produced by your visit will remain within the participating communities. For that reason, I invite you to become involved in this life project, because, even if you were not able to travel the Amazon basin, you still would do something good not just for Amazonian people and for our future generations.

In my case, I do not want to become yet another exploiter, profiting from Amazonia people. Thus, I am choosing to donate a major percentage of the profits of this book to recycle resources back into the area.

At the present time, I have chosen to donate and help the Nariño Hospital in the Colombian Amazon jungle. In addition, part of the profits will help the research department of the University of Amazon in the city of Benjamin Constant in Brazil. In addition, the book sales will benefit the people of Peru and the very needy community of Santa Rosa that is located in the middle of the jungle, bordering Colombia.

Please help protect and conserve the environment

Is This Book For You?

Again, I want to congratulate you for your decision to visit the Amazon basin home of Machu Picchu, the Amazon River and many more natural wonders as Iguazu and Angel falls; however, if you bought this book to plan your next deep expedition into the Amazon, then you might have the wrong book in your hands. You will need a book with a much deeper understanding of the jungle.

I wrote this book for ordinary people, who want to admire and discover the sheer beauty of the Amazon River, while enjoying a small trip to a single country or touring the whole river from beginning to end. It is also for grandparents who want to surprise their grandchildren with an unforgettable geography lesson that they will treasure forever.

This is for those who want to understand the mysticism developed by places that have remained virtually unchanged for thousands of years. This journey is also for women that want to be pampered by nature, while relating to wildlife creatures, such as the docile and fragile pink dolphins of the Amazon river or the Llamas in Machu Picchu. It is also an experience for young college students who want to hike alone to a "remote" part of the globe, while learning to dance to

Latin beats.

It is especially for those who want to discover the true beauty that exists within them. I guarantee it will be an experience beyond your wildest dreams in a safe and controlled environment.

Take the Challenge

Now here's a special invitation for you: I invite you to come and fall in love with some of the most beautiful and dazzling sunsets and sunrises on the planet whether you are in the Amazon river or in the Andean mountains.

This gorgeous destinations are waiting not just for you, but also for scientists, teachers, environmentalists, and entrepreneurs, but it is important to come before it is too late. Come and enjoy some of the most perplexing parts of the universe. What's more, this trip is a direct enticement to corporate manager, stressed by the complexities of the modern world.

Likewise, this is a call to action for those of you who keep watching National Geographic and Discovery Channel. I dare you to turn off the TV and come to live the adventure of your life in a safe, economical, and ecological environment. I invite you to see and experience the divinity of what God's hands are continuing to do every day. This trip to South America will make you shine in front of your friends.

Take advantage and bring your children to show them wonderful and strange creatures, like the turtle "Matamala" that cannot be seen in other parts of the planet. Friends, the world is asking you to come and experience these magnificent ancient places with the hope that you too would feel the pain of so many trees being cut.

Let your mind wander and be inspired by the simplicity of life; that is the key to happiness of Amazon people. Most likely you will discover the meaning of humbleness in this unexpected place while experiencing other intelligent ways of living. Hopefully you will be able to apply as you return home.

My Dear Friend, dreams do come true, and whether you are high up in the mountains or down in the flatlands of the Amazon forest, anything is possible. It is worth it, and all you need to do is to decide to come right now. I assure you that this trip has the power and ingredients to transform your life and bring new significance to your existence.

Tips About Reading This Book

For practical purposes, we will leave any city in USA and land in Lima, Peru. While you are in Lima, I highly recommend you to take advantage of the nightlife and exquisite gastronomy that this metropolis, of more than 9 million people, has to offer.

Machu Picchu & Amazon River

Then we will flight to Cuzco, the capital city of the Inca Empire and the oldest city in Latin America. Afterward, we will visit the Inca ruins in this imaginary journey. Next we will flight to the jungle city of Iquitos, one of the most powerful cities during the robber boom of the eighteen century.

From here, we would flight back to the Peruvian capital of Lima or we could keep navigating the mighty Amazon going true Colombia and Brazil until you reach the end of the river on the Atlantic Ocean.

Either way to go, it is going to be a wonderful trip, so lose your fears and grab your suitcase, because now is the time to begin our magical journey.

The recommendations that I make are based on my own travel experiences and those of many other travelers that I have met during my trips. One of the most important tips that I would give you right now is to have as much contact with the locals and befriend them, and they, in turn, will end up protecting you from the "undesirable" people that usually are well identified by the locals.

To make reading easier, we will use miles (mi) as the unit of measurement of distances and US dollars (US $) for all prices. Conversions were made at the official exchange rates at the end of 2011.

About Your Visa

Remember that you must have a valid passport for international travel, with the respective visas to enter the countries you plan to visit. Surely, you cannot get visas in the jungle towns; you must have them before your trip starts. Also, keep in mind that the citizens of the USA, Canada, Japan, and many other countries must obtain visas before entering Brazil. Therefore if you are planning to navigate downstream to the Atlantic ocean you must procure the respective visa at your hometown.

If you plan to stay in the tri-border area, this will not be required. Colombia and Peru, at present, do not require a visa for U.S. citizens, but it is highly recommended to check the conditions before leaving their country.

If you have your passport up to date and in good condition with the required visa, then your immigration and customs formalities will go very fast and pleasant.

Mainly, do not forget to bring the certificate of vaccination against yellow fever, as authorities will require it at the point of entry. However, malaria or any other vaccinations are not required and are not recommended.

Machu Picchu & Amazon River

HEADING TO PERU

Peru

Peru is a land of breathtaking mountain vistas, prehistoric ruins and the Amazon - perfect for a family adventure. Nowadays, you could explore the Amazon for few days in search of indigenous wildlife then head out to stunning Machu Picchu or the other way around. Either way, you will be building lifetime experiences that you will cherish for the rest of your life.

The easiest way to visit both wonders of the world is starting your trip in Lima, Peru's capital. From here, you could flight initially to Cuzco the gateway city for Machu Picchu and then flight to the jungle to Iquitos the most popular Amazon city. Alternatively, Pucalpa and Yurimaguas are also great Amazonian towns to visit. These jungle cities have excellent air and ground transportation with the exception of Iquitos that has not ground transportation from Lima.

But before we head out to Machu Picchu or the Amazonas, let us familiarize a bit with the fascinating and historical country of Peru.

Officially the Republic of Peru is a country in western South America. It is bordered on the north by Ecuador and Colombia, on the east by Brazil, on the southeast by Bolivia, on the south by Chile, and on the west by the Pacific Ocean.

Machu Picchu & Amazon River

Peruvian territory was home to the Norte Chico civilization, one of the oldest in the world and to the Inca Empire, the largest state in Pre-Columbian America.

The Spanish Empire conquered the region in the 16th century and established a Viceroyalty, which included most of its South American colonies. After achieving independence in 1821, Peru has undergone periods of political unrest and fiscal crisis as well as periods of stability and economic upswing.

Peru's geography varies from the arid plains of the Pacific coast to the peaks of the Andes mountains and the tropical forests of the Amazon Basin. It is a developing country with a high Human Development Index score and a poverty level around 31%. Its main economic activities include agriculture, fishing, mining and manufacturing of products such as textiles.

The Peruvian population, estimated at about 30 million, is multiethnic, including Amerindians, Europeans, Africans, and Asians. The main spoken language is Spanish, although a significant number of Peruvians speak Quechua or other native languages. This mixture of cultural traditions has resulted in a wide diversity of expressions in fields such as art, cuisine, literature, and music.

In this book, initially we will be heading to the glorious ruins of Machu Picchu, making the later part of our trip the Amazon River. In these fantastic places you will see birds soaring overhead and plenty of monkeys playing in the trees above, so bring your binoculars and do not forget your zoom lens.

For now, let just stay right here in Lima the capital city of Peru.

Lima

Lima is the capital and largest city of Peru. It is located in the valleys of the Chillón, Rímac and Lurín rivers, in the central part of the country, on a desert coast overlooking the Pacific Ocean. Together with the seaport of Callao, it forms a contiguous urban area known as the Lima Metropolitan Area. With a population fast approaching 9 million, Lima is the fifth largest city in Latin America. Lima is home to one of the largest financial hubs in Latin America.

Lima was founded by Spanish conquistador Francisco Pizarro on January 18, 1535, as la Ciudad de los Reyes, or "the City of Kings". It became the capital and most important city in the Spanish Viceroyalty of Peru. Following the Peruvian War of Independence, it became the capital of the Republic of Peru. Today, around one-third of the Peruvian population lives in the metropolitan area.

Peru's Highways.

Lima is a major stop on the Pan-American Highway. Because of its location on the country's central coast,

Machu Picchu & Amazon River

Lima is also an important junction in Peru's highway system. Three of the major highways originate in Lima.

The Northern Pan-American Highway, this highway extends more than 830 mi to the border with Ecuador connecting the northern districts of Lima with many major cities along the northern Peruvian coast. The Central Highway (Spanish: Carretera Central), this highway connects the eastern districts of Lima with many cities in central Peru.

The highway extends 530 mi with its terminus at the city of Pucallpa near Brazil. The Southern Pan-American Highway, this highway connects the southern districts of Lima to cities on the southern coast. The highway extends 900 mi to the border with Chile.

The city of Lima has one big bus terminal station located next to the mall Plaza Norte in the north of the city. This bus station is the point of departure and arrival of many buses with national and international destinations. There are other bus stations for each company around the city.

In addition, there are informal bus stations located in the south, center and north of the city; these bus stations are cheap but dangerous and are not recommended for foreigners.

Please help protect and conserve the environment

Public Transportation

Eighty percent of the city's history having occurred during the pre-automobile era, Lima's road network is based mostly on large divided avenues rather than freeways. In recent times however, Lima has developed a freeway network now made up of nine freeways.

The urban transport system is composed of over 652 transit routes, which are served, by buses, microbuses, and combis. The system is unorganized and is characterized by the lack of formality. The service is run by 464 private companies, which are poorly regulated by the local government. Fares average at around one sol or $0.30 USD. The city of Lima has also more than 100 km of cycle paths.

Taxis in the city are mostly informal; they are relatively cheap but could be dangerous. There are no meters so drivers are told the desired destination and the fare is agreed upon before the passenger enters the taxi. Taxis vary in sizes from small four door compacts to large vans. They are virtually everywhere, with different colors, accounting for a large part of the car stock. In many cases they are just a private car with a taxi sticker on the windshield. Additionally, there are several companies that provide taxi service on-call.

Automobiles, known as colectivos, render express service on some major roads of the Lima Metropolitan Area. The colectivos signal their specific destination with a sign on the their windshield. Their routes are not generally publicized, but are understood by frequent users. The cost is generally higher than public transport however they cover greater distances at greater speeds due to the lack of stops. This service is informal and is not allowed in the city. Some people in the periphery of the city use the so-called "mototaxi" for short distances

El Metropolitano

The Metropolitan Transportation System or El Metropolitano is a public transportation system, which integrate the Independent Corridor of Mass-Transit Buses known by its Spanish initials as COSAC. This system links the principal points of the Lima Metropolitan Area and the first phase of this project runs from the north of the city to Chorrillos in the south of the city. It began commercial operations on July 28th, 2010. This system is similar to the TransMilenio of Bogotá, Colombia.

Lima Metro

The Lima Metro, an above ground mass transit system, which 3rd phase of the Line One is already opened to public. There are six more lines in planning phase. Line 1's extension to the city's center was opened in July 2011, linking Villa el Salvador with downtown Lima in a matter of only thirty minutes, a trip that currently lasts one hour and forty minutes with other public transport system.

The Lima Metro has sixteen passenger stations, located at an average distance of 0.7 mi. It starts its path in the Industrial Park of Villa El Salvador, south of the city, continuing on to Av. Pachacútec in Villa María del Triunfo and then to Av. Los Héroes in San Juan de Miraflores. Afterwards, it continues through Av. Tomás Marsano in Surco to reach Ov. Los Cabitos and then on to Av. Aviación to finish in Av. Grau in the city center. Construction to extend Line 1 until its final destination, through Av. Próceres de la Independencia in San Juan de Lurigancho, is scheduled to begin shortly.

Reaching Lima by Air

Peru is mainly served by the Jorge Chávez International Airport, located in Callao (LIM). It is the largest airport of the country with the largest amount of domestic and international air traffic. It also serves as a major hub in the Latin American air network. Lima's Jorge Chavez International Airport is the fourth largest air hub in South America. The airport, however it is the base for the largest cargo hub in the continent.

Lima can be reached by air from practically anywhere in the world. Most airlines have direct flights to Peru, and here are some of the main Non-Stop routes:

Machu Picchu & Amazon River

FROM	TIME	AIRLINE
Amsterdam	12h 40m	KLM
Andahuaylas, Peru	1h 15m	LC Busre, Star Peru
Anta, Peru	1h 10m	LC Busre
Antofagasta, Chile	2h 54m	Sky Airline, TACA
Arequipa, Peru	1h 28m	LAN, TACA, StarPer
Asuncion, Paraguay	3h 40m	TACA
Atlanta, USA	6h 50m	Delta
Ayacucho, Peru	1h 0m	LC Busre, Star Peru
Bogotá	2h 56m	Avianca, LAN, TACA
Brasília, Brazil	4h 57m	LAN, TACA
Buenos Aires, Argentina	5h 3m	LAN, TACA, Aerolineas Argentinas
Cajamarca, Peru	1h 22m	LC Busre, LAN
Cancún, Mexico	5h 10m	LAN
Caracas, Venezuela	4h 15m	TACA, LAN
Chiclayo, Peru	1h 15m	LAN, TACA, StarPer
Córdoba, Argentina	3h 55m	LAN
Cuzco, Peru	1h 23m	LAN, StarPeru, TACA

Please help protect and conserve the environment

MYNOR SCHULT

Fort Lauderdale	5h 37m	Spirit
Guayaquil, Ecuador	1h 52m	TACA, LAN
Havana, Cuba	5h 15m	TACA
Houston, USA	6h 35m	United
Huanuco, Peru	0h 57m	LC Busre, Star Peru
Iguassu Falls, Brazil	4h 5m	LAN
Iquitos, Peru	1h 40m	LAN
Jauja, Peru	0h 42m	LC Busre, Star Peru
Juliaca, Peru	1h 40m	LAN
La Paz, Bolivia	1h 54m	TACA, LAN
Los Angeles, USA	8h 34m	LAN
Madrid, Spain	12h 6m	Iberia, LAN, Air Europa
Mexico City, Mexico	5h 48m	Aeromexico, LAN, TACA
Miami, USA	5h 42m	LAN, TACA
Montevideo, Uruguay	4h 45m	TACA
New York, USA	7h 46m	Continental, LAN

Machu Picchu & Amazon River

Panama	3h 28m	COPA
Paris, France	12h 15m	Air France
Piura, Peru	1h 30m	LAN, TACA
Porto Alegre, Brazil	4h 55m	TACA
Pucallpa, Peru	1h 5m	Star Peru
Dominican Republic	4h 55m	LAN
Quito, Ecuador	2h 15m	TACA, LAN
Rio de Janeiro, Brazil	5h 39m	TACA
Rosario, Argentina	4h 10m	LAN
San Francisco, USA	9h 25m	LAN
San Jose, Costa Rica	3h 45m	TACA
El Salvador	4h 20m	TACA
Santa Cruz, Bolivia	2h 32m	TACA, LAN
Santiago, Chile	4h 15m	LAN, TACA, Sky Air
Santo Domingo	4h 45m	TACA,
Sao Paulo, Brazil	5h 15m	TACA, LAN, TAM
Tacna, Peru	1h 50m	LAN

Please help protect and conserve the environment

Tarapoto, Peru	1h 15m	TACA, StarPeru, LAN
Toronto, Canada	7h 50m	Air Canada
Trujillo, Peru	1h 5m	LAN, TACA, StarPer
Tumbes, Peru	1h 45m	LAN

> Machu Picchu is by nature mysterious — and it has kept many researchers puzzled for years. They have used many myths and symbols left by the Inca culture to explain the position of many cities and fantastic temples in the Sacred Valley.

HEADING TO MACHU PICCHU

Arriving Cuzco

Cuzco, (10,750 ft), the oldest continuously inhabited city on the continent and the gateway city to Machu Picchu. It was the capital of the Inca Empire and considered by many Quechua peoples the spiritual center of the world. Much of colonial Cuzco was built on Inca foundations, and you would still see Inca stonework along the many streets. Make sure you visit the main square, the Cathedral, Santo Domingo Church, as well as a first introduction to Inca stonework at the ruins of Puka-Pukara, Qenqo, Tambo Machay, and the renowned fortress of Sacsayhuaman overlooking Cuzco and the surrounding valley.

The next day, as you are acclimatizing to the high altitude, take time to visit the towns of Pisac & Ollantaytambo. (or Ollanta as the locals called) It a full-day excursion to the village and ruins of Pisac located about 20 miles from Cuzco.

After exploring the ruins visit the colorful Indian market where you'll be able to trade with locals for a variety of handicrafts, including woolen sweaters and ponchos. Then visit the town and fortress of Ollantaytambo located in the Sacred Valley of the Incas.

Once you are ready to head to Machu Picchu, most people take an early train traveling from Cuzco to

Aguas Calientes, viewing the terraced farms and the villagers along the way. Make sure to take plenty of time to explore the ruins and take your own stunning photos of this archaeological wonder.

Reaching Cuzco By Air

Once you are in Lima you could practically leave for Cuzco, the gateway city to Machu Picchu, at any time since there is plenty of flights. Currently, several local airlines serve CUZCO; among them, STARPERU and LanPeru scheduled several daily flights every day. Many of them go directly to Iquitos or make a quick stop in their way to other cities.

Well-trained pilots and professional crews flight modern and comfortable Boeing jets 737s, with a capacity for more than 150 passengers. Due to the popularity of these routes, the prices are quite affordable, around $100 for any air flight between Lima and Cuzco or the other jungle cities. During low season, it's possible to obtain one-way tickets for less than $70.

Here's an important money-saving tip: If you purchase tickets for the Peruvian local flights in your hometown, whether the USA, Canada, or Europe, then you will most likely be paying about $300 extra for each segment. Therefore, my recommendation is that after buying your international air ticket, (do not pay more than $400 from your home city in America, $600 from Europe, or $800 from Asia and Oceania), visit the local airline websites that are listed at the end of this book and buy directly from those local airlines saving up to $500.

Reaching Cuzco By Bus

However, if you will like to see the most amazing views you should rather travel by bus. Therefore, from the central bus station in Lima, take a bus to Cuzco high in the Andean Mountains.

For most cities in the jungle, usually, the routes leading to them are in very poor condition and reaching those destinations may become true adventures. However the popular Lima-Cuzco route is very well maintained and serve by modern buses.

From Lima you could take one of the several bus companies that go to Cuzco. The trip takes approximately 24 hours. The bus fares from Lima to Cuzco range from 30 to 60 dollars. Mainly, there are two routes: one goes through Arequipa and the other through Puquio.

There are at least three reliable bus companies running the route Lima-Cuzco. One is Transportes Ormeño with a bus service called Royal Class at a cost of about 50 dollars one way. They provide breakfast, lunch and dinner, on-board movies, AC, clean wc, etc.

Another company is Cruz del Sur somewhat less expensive which the same service that Ormeno, but with older less comfortable equipment.   The less expensive seem to be Transportes Civa with a fare of about 25 dollars. Less comfortable with older buses.

It should be noted that it is worthwhile for such a long trip, to choose the cama (bed) option instead of the less comfortable semi-cama (semi-bed) fare. The difference is about 10 dollars, but half way there you will feel pretty smart that you took that option.

Buses to Machu Picchu

Most of the tourists take the train from Cuzco all the way to Aguas Calientes the closest town to Machu Picchu.

However, if you want to travel like the Peruvians and save half on transportation cost, from the Cuzco bus terminal take the bus to "Ollantaytambo" town. (Ollanta.)   The trip takes just about 2 hours. From Ollanta take the train to Aguas Calientes. There are several trains with the last one leaving as late as 8:00 PM and it cost close to 30 dollars each way.

Train fares are much more expensive from Cuzco (about 45 dollars each way) as most of tourists take the train there. However, the natives take the train in Ollanta at much lower fares.

Keep in mind that as the secret is out, the Ollanta train station is becoming more popular among tourist, so I highly recommend arriving early to make sure that there are still tickets available.

Upon train arrival to Machu Picchu, you would spent the night in Aguas Calientes, the town at the base of Machu Picchu mountain, then the next morning climb up to the pre-Hispanics ruins.

The buses up the hill start early and by 6:00 am you would be heading up to complete the final leg for this part of the journey. The bus cost approximately 8 dollars each way although my recommendation is to walk up the mountain if you are in good physical shape.

The entrance fee to Machu Picchu is about 150 soles or approximately 50 dollars, but with any student ID you will get a fifty percent discount.

If you feel like climbing it is best to start early and climb up to Huayna Picchu first and then down to the Machu Picchu ruin, since the ascent of Huayna Picchu is not allowed after 1:00 pm.

The "Lost City of the Incas" or Machu Picchu is set in the saddle of a mountain 1,000 feet above the Urubamba River, hidden form plain side view and probably one of the reasons why Machu Picchu escaped ransacking by the Spaniards.

Machu Picchu & Amazon River

Once you arrive you will be able to explore the walls, stairways, temples and terraces either by yourself or with a professional guide.

For the more energetic, a moderate 2-mile hike up to the Sun Gate offers fabulous views overlooking this ancient wonder.

Departures from Aguas Calientes to Machu Picchu
(Distance 8 km. Travel Time: 25 minutes)

Tramus S.A. +5184-211177
tramusa@latinmail.com

Waynapicchu S.A. +51-84-243972
waynapicchu@latinmail.com

Pachaqutek S.A. +51-84-9622436
pachakuteq64@latinmail.com

Tunqui S.A. +51-84-211278
tunqui@latinmail.com

Hot Warwe S.A. +51-84-211100
aguascalientes29@latinmail.com

MACHU PICCHU

Machu Picchu, Peru, is one of the major tourist destinations in the world, thanks to the magnificent architecture that presents the citadel, and the mystery surrounding its discovery and the fate of its inhabitants.

Accessible only by two roads, remains controlled entry of visitors to this cultural treasure of humanity. Machu Picchu, Peru, was one of the vacation homes of the first Inca emperor, Pachacuti (1438-1470). Some experts

Machu Picchu & Amazon River

> **IMPORTANT**
>
> The government has limited the number of visitors to Machu Picchu to just 2500 people per day. To avoid disappointment it is now essential to purchase your Machu Picchu entrance tickets well before arriving at Machu Picchu. The government have introduced an online booking system so tickets can be bought online at www.machupicchu.gob.pe

say that the citadel was dedicated to two functions, the residence and the religious shrine.

Machu Picchu ("Old Peak") is a pre-Columbian 15th-century Inca site located 7,970 ft above sea level. It is situated on a mountain ridge above the Urubamba Valley in Peru, which is 50 mi northwest of Cuzco and through which the Urubamba River flows.

Most archaeologists believe Machu Picchu was built as an estate for the Inca emperor Pachacuti. (1438–1472)

Often referred to as the "Lost City of the Incas", it is perhaps the most familiar icon of the Inca World.

The Incas started building the "estate" around AD 1400, but abandoned it as an official site for the Inca rulers a century later at the time of the Spanish Conquest. Although known locally, it was unknown to the outside world before being brought to international attention in 1911 by the American historian Hiram Bingham. Since then, Machu Picchu has become an important tourist attraction. Most of the outlying buildings have been reconstructed in order to give tourists a better idea of what the structures originally looked like. By 1976, thirty percent of Machu Picchu had been restored. The restoration work continues to this day.

Since the site was never known to the Spanish during their conquest, it is highly significant as a relatively intact cultural site. Machu Picchu was declared a Peruvian Historical Sanctuary in 1981 and a UNESCO World Heritage Site in 1983. In 2007, **Machu Picchu was voted one of the New Seven Wonders of the World** in a worldwide Internet poll.

Machu Picchu was built in the classical Inca style, with polished dry-stone walls. Its three primary buildings are the *Intihuatana*, the *Temple of the Sun*, and the *Room of the Three Windows*.

These are located in what is known by archaeologists as the *Sacred District* of Machu Picchu.

The town is considered World Heritage Site for its quality, is a masterpiece of architecture and engineer-

Machu Picchu & Amazon River

ing, making it one of the biggest tourist destinations in the world.

The climate is hot, humid during the day, and cool at night. The temperature ranges between 12-24 ° C.

The sanctuary of Machu Picchu, Peru is divided into two main sectors, agriculture and urban areas. The city is surrounded by agriculture. The main access road comes from Cuzco and crosses the crest of the hill, reaching the entrance, after passing through the area of the lookout, guard posts, barns and agricultural terraces.

The sanctuary consists of a citadel, consisting of palaces, temples, houses and stores, as well as religious buildings, whose main element to the mausoleums carved into the rock.

The buildings, plazas and platforms that form the urban sector, are interconnected by a system of narrow streets and trails, mostly in the form of steps, which cross the terraces along a longitudinal axis plane. In the

> Visiting Machu Picchu may be expensive. The entrance fee is about to $50; however, students with an ISIC card pay only 50%. With the train ticket from Cusco close to $100 round trip, the bus ticket to the site at $16 round trip and a night's accommodation… it easily adds up close to $200. However, it is well worth it!

Please help protect and conserve the environment

urban sector is the main platform, which is the main square, which divides the buildings into "up" and "down". From the urban sector is blocked the access to the sanctuary, with elements such as defensive wall and ditch wide, it was a dry moat that surrounded the whole, as a form of restricted ceremonial isolation, not as a military fortification.

There is evidence of the use of astronomical criteria and rituals in the construction of buildings. Some of them are aligned with the solar azimuth during the solstices.

The material used is granite-white and came from nearby quarries. The stone was worked with crowbars and bronze tools. The stones were smoothed with abrasive sand and stone. Nearly all floors of the buildings are rectangular. There are buildings of one, two and eight gates, which are located on one side of the rectangle.

It is also common to find buildings with only three walls, with a colonnade wall covering space missing. There were two types of rigging of the stonewalls: with mud mortar, and finely carved stone in the main building. Currently there are no roofs, but experts agree that they were two or four sided roofs.

Machu Picchu & Amazon River

The Inca Trail

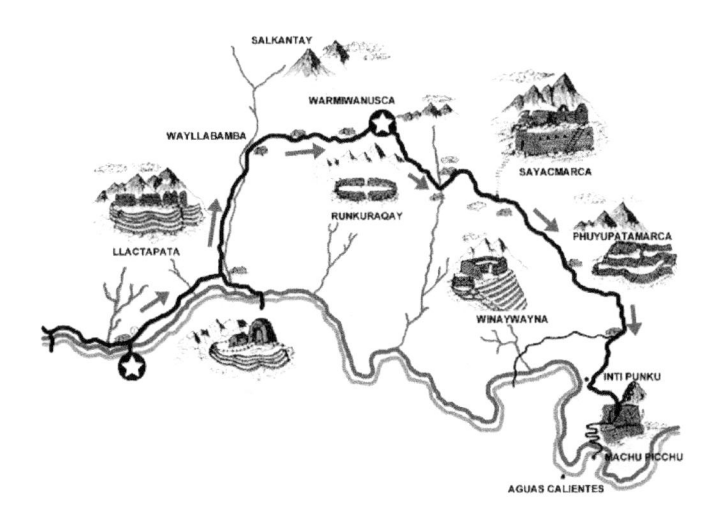

The Inca Trail between the Sacred Valley of the Urubamba River and the mysterious abandoned citadel of Machu Picchu is one of the world's classic treks. Climbing out of the river valley, crossing rugged mountain passes over 13,000 ft high, the trail winds through the Andes, passing numerous significant Inca ruins en route before descending through the Sun Gate to the silent stone city of Machu Picchu.

At its most basic, the Inca Trail (Camino del Inca) was a footpath through the Andes leading directly to the gates of Machu Picchu. Contrary to its image as a lone, lost, remote city, Machu Picchu was not isolated in the clouds. It was the crown of an entire Inca province, as ruins all along the Inca Trail attest. Machu Picchu was an administrative center in addition to its other presumed purposes. That larger purpose is comprehensible only to those who hike the ancient royal route and visit the other ruins scattered along the way to the sacred city.

More than that, though, the Incas conceived of Machu Picchu and the great trail leading to it in grand artistic and spiritual terms. Hiking the Inca Trail -- the ancient royal highway -- is, easily, the most authentic and scenic way to visit Machu Picchu and get a clear grasp of the Incas' overarching architectural concept and supreme regard for nature.

As impressive as Machu Picchu itself, the trail traverses a 125-sq.-mile national park designated as the Machu Picchu Historical Sanctuary. The entire zone is replete with extraordinary natural and man-made sights: Inca ruins, exotic vegetation and animals, and dazzling mountain and cloud forest vistas.

To hike the Inca Trail is a thrilling experience and a very great privilege. The purpose of this section is to share the thrill of the trip with those who may not have the privilege to do it personally and to help future hikers plan their coming adventure.

Today the Inca Trail -- which, as part of the Machu Picchu Historical Sanctuary, has been designated a World Heritage natural and cultural site -- is the most

Machu Picchu & Amazon River

important and most popular hiking trail in South America, followed by many thousands of ecotourists and modern-day pilgrims in the past 3 decades.

Its popularity in recent years -- more than 75,000 people a year hike the famous trail -- led to concerns among environmentalists and historians that the trail was suffering potentially irreparable degradation.

The National Institute of Culture (INC) and the Ministry of Industry, Tourism, Integration, and International Trade (MITINCI), reacting to pressure from groups such as UNESCO, which threatened to rescind Machu Picchu's World Heritage Site status, instituted far-reaching changes in practices designed to limit the number of visitors and damage to Machu Picchu and the Inca Trail.

Therefore, respect the ancient trail and its environment. Whatever you pack in, you must also pack out.

Basically, there are two ways to walk to Machu Picchu: either along a fairly arduous 4-day/3-night path with three serious mountain passes, or as part of a more recently opened and more accessible 2-day/1-night trail. You can hire porters to haul your packs or suck it up and do it the hard way. Independent trekking on the Inca Trail without an official guide has been prohibited since 2001. You must go as part of an organized group arranged by an officially sanctioned tour agency. A couple or a small number of people can organize their own group if they are willing to pay higher prices for the luxury of having their privacy.

Even with the new regulations, hiking the Inca Trail, beautiful and mystical as it is for most, is not a silent, solitary walk in the clouds. At least in high season, you will contend with groups walking the trail both in front of and behind you. Some will invariably be noisy student groups.

Furthermore, the Inca Trail is much more than a great hike. It is one small portion of an incredible network of such trails crossing high stony mountain ranges, bleak deserts, and raging Andean rivers, tying the Inca Empire together. At its peak expansion, Tahuantinsuyo --"The Four Corners", as the empire was known-- extended from what is now southern Colombia in the north, to central Chile in the south, a distance of about 3400 mi.

To rule such a vast domain, the emperor, or *Inca*, forged a remarkable communications system of approximately 18,600 mi of trails, paved through much its length, stepped where need be, through tunnels where necessary, and using gossamer suspension bridges built of straw ropes to cross rivers in the wet season.

The roads served to move the conquering Inca armies, and were generally wide enough for a minimum of two warriors to travel abreast. A system of runners stationed at rest houses known as *tambos* sped messages along the roadways, much like the Pony Express mail of the old American West. The *Inca* in his empire's capital at Cuzco could receive news from far away Quito, Ecuador's capital, as rapidly as a letter crosses between the two cities in today's mail.

As remarkable as this highway system was in the days when it was built, used and maintained, it is an astounding testimony to its construction that so many segments remain serviceable today, after half a millennium of neglect. Clearly, the Inca highway system ranks as one of the greatest engineering achievements of pre-industrial man.

Trekkers of the Inca Trail, be it the well-known portion leading to Machu Picchu, or lesser-visited segments, are privileged to make use of an archeological treasure, as well as to partake of scenes of surpassing beauty. Care for the trail: don't abuse it in ways that promote loosening or erosion of the stonework. Care for the beauty of the landscape: don't leave trash or waste behind.

From the Sacred Valley to Machu Picchu

Most Inca Trail treks begin at either Km. 88 (mile marker at 55 mi) on the railroad to Machu Picchu, or the village of Chilca, which lies in the Urubamba Valley downstream from Ollantaytambo, to which it is connected by a dirt road.

If beginning at mile marker Km 88, you have to take the mixed local train, since the first class tourist trains do not stop here. Be prepared to jump off quick, as even the mixed local train doesn't stop long. Here you cross the Urubamba on a footbridge at about 7200 ft and pay the 50 dollars entry fee for the Inca Trail. The trail turns back to the left and heads for the ruin known as Llactapata; there is a 1 km long side trail off to the right that will take you to a little visited ruin known as Q'ente o "hummingbird".

Beginning at Chilca, the trail, which here is an unpaved trail of possibly Inca or post-Inca origin, follows along the left bank of the Urubamba gorge, with views across the river of terraced farmland, snow-capped mountains, a glacial valley with a beautiful example of a terminal moraine, and a small, inhabited Inca ruin. For much of the nine kilometers from Chilca to Llactapata the rail line is also in sight on the opposite side of the river.

At Llactapata, there is a fine campsite near the ruins, popular with trekkers starting from Chilca. In '91 a family living in a house here was pleased to sell bottled drinks to hikers. Llactapata translated, as "town on a hillside" may be unimportant compared to Machu Picchu, but would be considered a major archeological site anywhere in North America and is well worth exploring it for a couple of hours. There are extensive agricultural terraces, ruined houses, and an unusual round watchtower-like structure

Machu Picchu & Amazon River

From Llactapata the trail turns south, away from the Urubamba and up the valley of the *Río Cusichacha*, a small stream scarcely deserving the appellation "river".

Trekkers starting from Km 88 will probably continue past Llactapata up the Cusichacha about seven km to its junction with the *Río Llullucha*, where the trail turns west and follows the Llullucha. Just above the junction of the two streams is the village of Huayllabamba ("grassy plain", the only inhabited village on the Inca Trail).

Beyond this village are three regular campsites along the *Río Llullucha*. The first of these is "Three White Stones" and is only about a half-hour walk from Huayllabamba. The next campsite, Llulluchapampa, is significantly higher up the trail, and colder, but features toilets. A third and final campsite on this side of the first high pass is yet another 20 minutes or half hour further up the trail. Any one of these campsites makes a good overnight rest stop for trekkers starting from Km. 88. Llulluchapampa camp is about 11 km from Llactapata.

From the campsites in the Llullucha valley, the Inca Trail struggles up above the tree line to cross the first and highest of the mountain passes between Llactapata and Machu Picchu. At Huarmiwañusqa, more popularly known as "Dead Woman Pass", the trail reaches an elevation of 13,772 ft. It's a heart-pounder for most, but the reward is a stunning view back down the Llullucha valley to snow-capped mountains in the distance and a preview of the ups and downs ahead on the trail to Runkurakay.

From Dead Woman Pass, the descent to the small stream known as the *Río Pacamayo* requires an hour or more. A short distance below the pass the trail passes through the first tunnel, under and between giant boulders. From the *Río Pacamayo* a new ascent ensues, which brings one to the small ruin of Runkurakay. This name, translated variously as "oval hut" or "egg hut" is the smallest and most enigmatic of the ruins along the hike. Perhaps it was a watchtower or a small *tambo* for messenger relays. In any case, hard by the ruin is a pleasant campsite. The distance from Llulluchapampa to Runkurakay is only about six km, but getting up and over the pass is strenuous due to the high altitude.

Just above Runkurakay, the Inca Trail becomes paved with stones and assumes the more engineered nature for which it is justly famed, and which characterizes it from here to Machu Picchu.

A short hike beyond Runkurakay ruin brings one to the pass of the same name, at 13,116 ft, and after another hour's downhill hike, one arrives at the ruin of Sayacmarca or "dominant town". This fort-like ruin lies to the left of the trail and must be reached by climbing 98 steep stone steps. The town or fort is built on a mountain spur and commands fine views.

Machu Picchu & Amazon River

From near Sayacmarca the paved trail can be seen stretching away into the distance. A short distance along the trail below Sayacmarca is another smaller ruin and possible camping area.

In the stretch of Inca Trail between Sayacmarca and the next major ruin, Phuyupatamarca, trekkers will find some of the most impressive Inca trail engineering. Along one section, the trail passes through a boggy area as a raised causeway. At another point, it passes through a hewn tunnel, and at yet another point stones were set in notches cut in a cliff face to build up a surface wide enough to walk along. This section of the trail also features some of the most interesting exotic vegetation seen on the trek, and at one point, an awesome view back down to the *Río Urubamba* in its winding gorge.

After passing through the third pass at 13,125 ft and some of the wildest rugged scenery imaginable, the trail reaches Phuyupatamarca ("town above the clouds"), approximately nine km and two to three hours hike from Sayacmarca. The ruin is reached by descending a long flight of stairs, and near the entry, the trekker finds a series of six flowing liturgical fountains or "baths", illustrating the Incas' love of sparkling, splashing water and engineering ability to play with it. Near Phuyupatamarca is a popular campsite, and if the weather is clear, from a ridgecrest above the ruin a spectacular view can be had of mighty Salcantay

20,694 ft, a sacred mountain to the Incas. Altogether, the town above the clouds is a most intriguing site.

The remaining distance to Machu Picchu is around ten km, including a short side trip to Wiñay Wayna ruins, and mainly downhill, dropping from 11,975 ft to a mere 7875 ft at Machu Picchu. The change in vegetation from alpine bunchgrass to relatively densely forested mountainsides is dramatic.

Leaving Phuyupatamarca the Inca Trail descends an unbelievably long series of winding steps, many cut into the living rock. Amazingly, enough, this section of the trail was only discovered a few years ago, and opened to trekkers in 1985; formerly, hikers followed a section of non-Inca trail between Phuyupatamarca and Wiñay Wayna. One has to wonder what unknown archeological treasures remain hidden in the underbrush.

After a two-and-a-half hour hike, the somewhat surprisingly located Trekker Hotel is reached. Beds, floor space for sleeping bags, hot showers, meals and drinks are available. And here a side trail takes off a half a kilometer to Wiñay Wayna, named after an orchid species call forever young. This lovely ruin is considered by some to be more beautiful than Machu Picchu, if not as dramatic.

It consists of an upper ceremonial section, and a lower living section, connected by a long set of steps paralleling a beautiful series of ten liturgical fountains.

Machu Picchu & Amazon River

Both sections are flanked by an enormous sweeping amphitheatre of agricultural terraces, and the entire scene is set off by a waterfall in the forested backdrop. This site alone would justify the entire Inca Trail hike.

From the Trekker Hotel, a two-hour hike, the trail passing through densely forested mountain slopes, brings one to the *Intipunku* or Sun Gate, and a first, unforgettable view of the ultimate goal: Machu Picchu.

Moreover, from here it is just a 30-minute hike along the broad, flagstone-paved trail to reach the Watchman's Hut in the upper part of the Machu Picchu's Agricultural Sector. But savor the shifting panoramas as you hike this final segment of the Inca Trail: the shear bromeliad-studded cliffs to the right of the trail; what look like toy trains and tracks far below in the sinuous gorge of the Urubamba; the drama of Huayna Picchu peak rising like a stone juggernaut out of Pachamama's breast; and the mysterious grey stone city mounted like a gem in a setting of cliffs and canyons. There is no other place comparable!

Practical Information for Trekkers:

The number of hikers allowed to trek the Inca Trail is strictly regulated and space is limited. For this reason, most outfitters supplying Inca Trail trek services require reservations more than a month in advance. Inca Trail permits are issued for each individual trekker by name, and must be obtained at least 30 days before the day the trek commences.

To enjoy the Inca Trail to the fullest, you should allow four days for the trek. Shorter treks are possible, but not ideal.

The number of users on the Inca trail is restricted by limiting trail entry to 500 per day. this figure includes visiting trekkers and support personnel such as guides, cooks and porters. Since the support personnel outnumber the visitors, the actual number of entry permits available for visitors is less than 250 per day.

The cost of the Inca trail entry permit is about 98 dollars for the full Inca trail; this includes entry to Machu Picchu. For the one-day hike from km 104 to Machu Picchu via Wiñay Wayna, the entry fee is only about 75 dollars.

Inca trail permits must be paid in full within 24 hrs of booking and to acquire a trail permit the trekker must supply the following information: full name exactly as it appears in your passport; passport number; nationality; and date of birth. This trail permits are personal, and they are non-refundable. It cannot be modified once it's booked and cannot be transferred to another visitor.

Machu Picchu & Amazon River

The Inca trail permit is only good for four days of trail use. Please take in consideration that five day treks are no longer available.

As I have mentioned demand for Inca trail trek permits is now high throughout the year, especially during the summer months of June through September when demand for trek permits regularly exceeds the number of spaces available. Needless to say, that booking as early as possible is necessary to avoid disappointments.

No one is allowed to trek the Inca trail independently as the you must have a guide and use porters.

Porters cannot be asked to carry over 44 lbs total.

Pack light for the trek. There is a weight limit for your personal gear to be carried by the porters. the limit is 20 lbs per person and anything over the weight you have to carry yourself.

Items Need for the Trip

- Backpack: full-size backpack needed only if you are carrying in excess of 20 lbs gear weight; however, if you do not exceed this amount then you only need a daypack.
- Tent, sleeping bag and compact sleeping mat. Generally, the trekking agency in charge of your Inca Trail trek will probably provide most of this equipment. However, you need to check with them to be certain what they provide it. Some trekkers prefer to bring their own sleeping bags. Accordingly, some agencies provide the tents and sleeping pads, but they will also rent sleeping bags with clean liners.
- Clothing you can layer for different temperatures at different altitudes: two-piece polypro long johns are good; an alpaca sweater for an outer layer is good. One complete change of clothing so you can get into dry clothes if what you are wearing gets soaked.
- Lightweight raingear; if jacket can double as a windbreaker, this is doubly good.
- Lightweight, but good quality hiking boots that provide ankle support. Make sure you break them in before your Inca trail hike.
- Cap or hat with brim for sun protection; sunglasses; strong sunblock.
- Multipurpose knife, flashlight and extra batteries, matches.
- Water bottle and water purifying kit.

- Towel and necessary toiletries, including toilet paper.
- Bug repellent just in case you need it.
- A great digital Camera.
- Essential first aid items.
- If you are not traveling with an organized group with porters and cook, you will have to carry all your own food and cookgear.

When to go

Peruvian climate features two seasons: dry season from May through September and wet season from October through April.

In the dry season, the high Andean countryside is characterized by sere brown, gold and tan colors, overarched by clear blue skies and puffy white clouds. While there is some rain in the dry season, it is not generally enough to impede hiking or road transport. The wet season is warmer, and the mountainsides are a fantastic variety of verdant shades; flowers abound. Nevertheless, the skies tend to be overcast, misty, and sweeping views of the ranges may be hard to find. Rainfall can be heavy and abundant, causing landslides that impede travel on mountain roads and railroads and flights are commonly delayed by weather.

Trekking in the mountains and canoeing on Andean or jungle rivers during the wet season is generally less enjoyable than in the dry, though much depends on your luck with the weather on the particular days you are hiking.

For the Inca Trail, May might be the best month as it is the end of the wet season, when the rains have quit, the skies are clear and views are great, but everything is still bright and green. The disadvantage of going in the best weather months is that this is precisely when traffic is highest on the trail. The advantages of the wet season include fewer trekkers to share the trail with, and, naturally, water is easier to find!

Group size may not exceed 16 visitors, with a support crew of 22 for a total of 38 persons.

Groups may not stay more than four nights on that portion of the Inca Trail that lies within the Machu Picchu sanctuary.

The trail is closed one month each year for maintenance generally in January or February.

Preparing for Your Trek

The classic 4-day route is along hand-hewn stone stairs and trails through sumptuous mountain scenery and amazing cloud forest, past rushing rivers and dozens of Inca ruins. The zone is inhabited by rare orchids, 419 species of birds, and even the indigenous spectacled bear.

The trek begins at Qorihuayrachina near Ollantaytambo -- more easily described as Km 88 of the railway from Cuzco to Aguas Calientes. The 26-mile route passes three formidable mountain passes, including the punishing "Dead Woman's Pass," to a maximum altitude of 13,800 ft.

Most groups enter the ruins of Machu Picchu at sunrise on the fourth day, although others, whose members are less keen on rising at 3:30am to do it, trickle in throughout the morning.

The 2-day version of the trail is being promoted by authorities as the Camino Sagrado del Inca, or "Sacred Trail," although it might also be called the Camino "Lite." It is a reasonable alternative to the classic trail if time or fitness is lacking.

The path rises only to an elevation of about 9,020 ft. and is a relatively easy climb to Huiñay Huayna and then down to Machu Picchu. The minitrail begins only 9 miles away from Machu Picchu, at Km 104, and it circumvents much of the finest mountain scenery and ruins. Groups spend the night near the ruins of Huiñay Huayna before arriving at Machu Picchu for sunrise on the second day.

Either way you go, it is advisable to give yourself a couple of days in Cuzco or a spot in the Sacred Valley to acclimatize to the high elevation.

The cost of hiking the trail has steadily climbed – and the Standard-class 4-day treks now cost $400 including entrance fees and return by tourist trail.

Independent trekkers generally join a mixed group of travelers; groups tend to be between 12 and 16 people, with guaranteed daily departures. The cost includes a bus to Km 88 to begin the trek, an English-speaking guide, tents, mattresses, three daily meals, and porters who carry all common equipment. Tips for porters or guides are extra. Personal porters, to carry your personal items, can be hired for about $50 for the 4 days.

Premium-class services generally operate smaller group sizes to a maximum of 10 trekkers, and you generally get an upgrade on the return train. Prices for premium group treks, organized for private groups, range from $500 to as high as $1,000 per person.

Prices vary for trail packages based on services and the quality and experience of the agency. In general, you get what you pay for. Rock-bottom prices will probably get you a guide who speaks little English, food that is barely edible, camping equipment on its last legs, and a large, rowdy group. Especially important is the ability of an agency to guarantee departure even if its desired target number of travelers is not filled.

Machu Picchu & Amazon River

To guarantee a spot with an agency, which must request a trek permit for each trekker, it is imperative that you make a reservation with enough advance. You'd be wise to do this at least 3 months or more in advance, if you plan to go during peak months of May through October.

Reservations can be made as much as a year in advance. Gone are the days when trekkers could simply show up in Cuzco and organize a trek on the fly. Changing dates once you have a reservation is difficult, if not impossible. If spots remain on agency rosters, they are offered on a first-come, first-served basis.

The entrance ticket for the 2-day Camino Sagrado, purchased in Cuzco, is $50 for adults and $27 for students. Basic pooled service (maximum 16 trekkers) costs about $150 per person, including the entrance fee. There are no premium-class services for the 2-day trek.

Howling at the Moon -- For a truly spectacular experience on the Inca Trail, plan your trip to depart 2 or 3 days before a full moon. Locals say the weather's best then, and having your nights illuminated by a full or near-full moon, especially for the early rise and push into Machu Picchu on the last day, is unforgettable.

Inca Trail Tour Agencies

Only officially sanctioned travel agencies are permitted to organize group treks along the Inca Trail, but do not worry there are at least 140 tour operators that have been granted government licenses to sell and operate Inca Trail treks.

With the higher-end agencies, it is usually possible to assemble your own private group, with as few as two hikers. Budget trekkers will join an established group. In addition to cost, hikers should ask about group size (12 or fewer is best; 16 is the most allowed), the quality of the guides and their English-speaking abilities, the quality of food preparation, and porters and equipment. You should also make certain that the agency guarantees daily departures so that you're not stuck waiting in Cuzco for a group to be assembled.

Recommended agencies that score high on those criteria follow. Keep in mind that the addresses and phone numbers may change frequently and nowadays their websites are more reliable sources of information.

Amazon River Expert, Murrieta, CA (1 858 222 1077 www.AmazonRiverExpert.com) A well-thought-of outdoors operator running high end private tours to Machu Picchu as well as numerous other programs in Lat-

Machu Picchu & Amazon River

in America. They specialize in low impact and sustainable tours in Colombia, Costa Rica, Peru and the Amazon.

Andean Life, Plateros 372 (tel. 084/221-491; www.andeanlife.com). A reputable midrange company offering both pooled basic and premium private treks with good guides.

Andean Treks, Av. Pardo 705 (tel. 800/683-8148 in the U.S. and Canada or 084/225-701 in Cuzco; www.andeantreks.com). A longtime (since 1980), Watertown, Massachusetts, running 5-day treks along the Inca Trail as well as numerous other programs in Latin America.

Andina Travel, Plazoleta Santa Catalina 219 (tel. 084/251-892; www.andinatravel.com). An upstart, progressive company interested in sustainable development, owned by a Cuzco native and his North American business partner.

Big Foot Tours, Triunfo 392, 2nd level (tel. 084/991-3851; fax 084/222-123; www.bigfootCuzco.com). A popular budget agency.

Chaska Tours, Garcilaso 265, 2nd floor #6 (tel. 084/240-424; www.chaskatours.com). A very capable midrange company, run by a Dutch and Peruvian team, praised for its private and group treks to Machu Picchu as well as Choquequirao.

Enigma, Jr. Clorinda Matto de Turner, 100 Urbanización Magisterial 1 Etapa (tel. 084/221-155; fax 084/221-153; www.enigmaperu.com). A relatively new adventure travel operator with a good reputation and specialized and alternative hiking and trekking options, good for small-group and private treks.

Explorandes, Av. Garcilaso 316-A (tel. 084/238-830; fax 084/233-784; www.explorandes.com). One of the top high-end agencies and the most experienced in treks and mountaineering across Peru. Especially good for forming very small private groups.

Inca Explorers, Ruinas 427 (tel. 084/241-070; fax 084/239-669; www.incaexplorers.com). One of the best agencies, offering midrange, comfortable Inca Trail treks. Porters carry hikers' packs, and groups are small (including private group treks).

Mayuc, Portal de Confiturías 211, Plaza de Armas (tel. 866/777-9213 in the U.S. and Canada or 084/242-824 in Cuzco; www.mayuc.com). Especially good for pampered Inca Trail expeditions (porters carry all packs). It aims to be low impact, and hosts smaller groups.

Q'Ente, Garcilaso 210 (tel. 084/222-535; fax 084/222-535; www.qente.com). Receives very high marks from budget travelers. It's very competitively priced, with responsible, good guides, and offers a premium trek with a maximum of eight trekkers.

SAS Adventure Travel, Portal de Panes 167 (Plaza de Armas; tel. 084/255-205; fax 084/225-757;

www.sastravelperu.com). Large, long-established agency serving budget-oriented trekkers. Very popular, responsible, and well organized.

United Mice, Plateros 351 (tel. 084/221-139; www.unitedmice.com). Started by one of the trail's most respected guides, this is another of the top agencies organizing affordable midrange treks.

Inca Trail Regulations

For decades, individuals trekked the Inca Trail on their own, but hundreds of thousands of visitors -- as many as 75,000 a year -- left behind so much detritus that not only was the experience compromised for most future trekkers, but the very environment was also placed at risk.

The entire zone has suffered grave deforestation and erosion. The Peruvian government, under pressure from international organizations, has finally instituted changes and restrictions designed to lessen the human impact on the trail and on Machu Picchu itself. While in the first couple of years, regulations were poorly enforced, today they are fully and strictly impose.

These changes have cut the number of trekkers on the trail in half and have made reservations essential in high season. Travelers willing to wing it might still find available spots a couple of days before embarking on the trail, perhaps even at discounted rates, but waiting is a huge risk if you're really counting on doing the Inca Trail.

The key changes for travelers are that it is no longer possible to go on the trail independently and no longer dirt-cheap to walk 4 days to Machu Picchu. The good news is that the trail is more organized and we now have much hope for its preservation.

"Coming straight up from Lima and getting stuck into the Inca Trail will leave even the fittest hiker gasping for air. With the 4200m "Dead Woman's Pass" waiting for you on day two of the four day hike, try to allow for a couple of days in nearby Cusco to acclimatise to the altitude before setting off." by Escaped to Peru

Machu Picchu & Amazon River

Day-by-Day: Classic 4-Day Inca Trek

The following is typical of the group-organized 4-day/3-night schedule along the Inca Trail.

Day 1 -- Trekkers arrive from Cuzco, either by train, getting off at the midway stop, Ollantaytambo, or Km 88; or by bus, at Km 82, the preferred method of transport for many groups. Starting at Km 82 doesn't add an appreciable distance to the trail. After crossing the Río Urubamba (Vilcanota), the first gentle ascent of the trail looms to Inca ruins at Llaqtapata. Also called Patallacta, here is where Bingham and his team first camped on the way to Machu Picchu. The path then crosses the Río Cusicacha, tracing the line of the river until it begins to climb and reaches the small village. the only one still inhabited along the trail, of Huayllabamba -- a 2- to 3-hour climb. Most groups spend their first night at campsites here. Total distance: 10 to 11km (6 1/4-6 3/4 miles).

Day 2 -- Is the hardest of the trek. The next ruins are at Llullucharoc (3,800m/12,460 ft.), about an hour's steep climb from Huayllabamba. Llulluchapampa, an isolated village that lies in a flat meadow, is a strenuous 90-minute to 2-hour climb through cloud forest. There are extraordinary valley views from here. Next up is the dreaded Abra de Huarmihuañusqa, or Dead Woman's Pass, the highest point on the trail and infamous among veterans of the Inca Trail. The air is thin, and the 4,200m (13,780-ft.) pass is a killer for most: a punishing 2 1/2-hour climb in the hot sun, which is replaced by cold winds at the top. It's not uncommon for freezing rain or even snow to meet trekkers atop the pass. After a deserved rest at the summit, the path descends sharply on complicated stone steps to Pacamayo (3,600m/11,810 ft.), where groups camp for the night. Total distance: 11km (6 3/4 miles).

Day 3 -- By the third day, most of the remaining footpath is the original work of the Incas, as in previous sections, the government "restored" some of the stonework. In route to the next mountain pass (1 hr.), trekkers encounter the ruins of Runcuracay. The circular structure (the name means, "basket shaped") is unique among those found along the trail. From here, a steep 45-minute to 1-hour climb leads to the second pass, Abra de Runcuracay (3,900m/12,790 ft.), and the location of an official campsite just over the summit. There are great views of the Vilcabamba mountain range. After passing through a naturally formed tunnel, the path leads past a lake and a stunning staircase to Sayacmarca (3,500m/11,480 ft.), named for its nearly inaccessible setting surrounded by dizzying cliffs. Among the ruins are ritual baths and a terrace viewpoint overlooking the Aobamba Valley, suggesting that the site was not inhabited but instead served as a rest-

Machu Picchu & Amazon River

ing point for travelers and as a control station. The trail backtracks a bit on the way to Conchamarca, another rest stop. Here, the well-preserved Inca footpath drops into jungle thick with exotic vegetation, such as lichens, hanging moss, bromeliads, and orchids, and some of the area unique bird species. After passing through another Inca tunnel, the path climbs gently for 2 hours along a stone road, toward the trail's third major pass.

Phuyupatamarca (3,800m/12,460 ft.); the final climb is considerably easier than the two that came before it. This is a spectacular section of the trail, with great views of the Urubamba Valley. Some of the region's highest snowcapped peaks (all over 5,500m/18,040 ft.), including Salcantay, are clearly visible, and the end of the trail is in sight. The tourist town of Aguas Calientes lies below, and trekkers can see the peak of Machu Picchu.

From the peak, trekkers reach the beautiful, restored Inca ruins of Phuyupatamarca. The ancient village is another one aptly named: It translates as "Town above the Clouds." The remains of six ceremonial baths are clearly visible, as are retaining-wall terraces. A stone staircase of 2,250 steps plummets into the cloud forest, taking about 90 minutes to descend.

The path forks, with the footpath on the left leading to the fan-shaped Intipata terraces. On the right, the trail pushes on to the extraordinary ruins of Huiñay Huayna, which are actually about a 10-minute walk from the trail. Back at the main footpath, there's a campsite and ramshackle trekker's hostel offering hot showers, food, and drink. The grounds are a major gathering place for trekkers before the final push to Machu Picchu, and for some, they're a bit too boisterous and unkempt, an unpleasant intrusion after all the pristine beauty up to this point on the trail. Although it's closest to Machu Picchu, the Huiñay Huayna ruins, nearly the equal of Machu Picchu, were only discovered in 1941. Its name, which means "Forever Young," refers not to its relatively recent discovery, but to the perpetually flowering orchid of the same name that is found in abundance nearby. The stop was evidently an important one along the trail; on the slopes around the site are dozens of stone agricultural terraces, and 10 ritual baths, which still have running water, awaited travelers. Total distance: 15km (9 1/3 miles).

Day 4 -- From Huiñay Huayna, trekkers have but one goal remaining: reaching Intipunku (the Sun Gate) and descending to Machu Picchu, preferably in time to witness the dramatic sunrise over the ruins. Most groups depart camp at 4am or earlier to reach the pass at Machu Picchu and arrive in time for daybreak, around 6:30am. Awaiting them first, though, is a good 60- to 90-minute trek along narrow Inca stone paths, and then a final killer: a 50-step, nearly vertical climb. The descent from Intipunku to Machu Picchu takes about 45 minutes.

Machu Picchu & Amazon River

Having reached the ruins, trekkers have to exit the site and deposit their backpacks at the entrance gate near the hotel. There, they also get their entrance passes to Machu Picchu stamped; the pass is good for 1 day only. Total distance: 7km (4 1/3 miles).

About Tipping

At the end of the Inca Trail, guides, cooks, and especially porters expect -- and fully deserve -- to be tipped for their services. They get comparatively little of the sum hikers pay to form part of the group, and they depend on tips for most of their salary. Please, tip to the extent that you are able.

> *"It was strangely like war. They attacked the forest as if it were an enemy to be pushed back from the beachheads, driven into the hills, broken into patches, and wiped out. Many operators thought they were not only making lumber but liberating the land from the trees..."*
>
> *Murray Morgan*

Please help protect and conserve the environment

Alternatives to the Inca Trail

The Inca Trail was once very much off the beaten path and at the cutting edge of adventure travel, for hard-core trekkers only. Although the Peruvian government has adopted new measures to restrict the numbers of trekkers along the trail, it has become so popular and well-worn that in high season it's become tough, if not impossible, to find the solitude and quiet contemplation such a sacred path deserves.

Trekkers and travelers looking for more privacy, authenticity, or bragging rights are seeking alternatives, and many adventure-travel companies are catering to this sector by offering other, less accessible trails to keep ahead of the masses on road less travelled or better said more comfortably traveled.

There are several international operators offering custom-designed alternatives to the traditional Inca Trail.

Adventure Life (tel. 800/344-6118; www.adventurelife.com) promotes a 10-day "Cachiccata Trek:

The Inca Trail Less Traveled"; Andean Treks (tel. 800/683-8148; www.andeantreks.com) suggests a 4-day "Moonstone to Sun Temple" trek, as well as others like the 6-day "Vilcanota Llama Trek".

Machu Picchu & Amazon River

Mountain Travel Sobek (tel. 888/687-6235; www.mtsobek.com) offers a 12-day and 7 days hiking the "other Inca Trails"

Wilderness Travel (tel. 800/368-2794; www.wildernesstravel.com) has a 12-day (6 days hiking) "Salcantay to Machu Picchu Hidden Inca Trail" tour. Prices range from about $550 to $3,800 per person.

The trend toward luxury, or soft, adventure is also gaining traction in the Peruvian Andes, and companies offering treks to Machu Picchu are targeting more affluent and creature comfort-oriented travelers who want the adventure experience without roughing it too much.

Mountain Lodges of Peru (tel. 084/236-069; www.mountainlodgesofperu.com), a new trekking company, has constructed four small "first quality" lodges on private lands in the Vilcabamba mountain range west of the Sacred Valley. The inns are stunning, not only for their locations but also their sophisticated architecture and amenities -- which include whirlpools, fireplaces, and sleek dining rooms.

Mountain Lodges offers its own 6-day treks starting at $2,500 per person, culminating in a visit to Machu Picchu, but the company has also contracted with international trekking and adventure companies, including Backroads (tel. 800/462-2848; www.backroads.com), Wilderness Travel, and Mountain Travel Sobek, which feature the lodges in their own 11-day "Machu Picchu Lodge to Lodge" or "Inn to Inn" packages. Prices run to $4,795 per person.

If the notion of luxury adventure travel or the possibility of running into someone you know is too much, you may want to skip Machu Picchu altogether or at least the idea of trekking there.

Alternative treks to Salcantay, Vilcabamba, or Choquequirao, the last a "lost" Inca city only truly unearthed in the past decade that takes 5 days to get to over an arduous trail, are increasingly offered by local trek tour agencies in Cuzco (such as Q'Ente or Enigma) and even some of the bigger international trekking companies.

Andean Lodges (tel. 084/224-613; www.andeanlodges.com), a joint initiative between the tour group Auqui Mountain Spirit and local Quechua shepherding communities, recently opened four new, ecofriendly mountain lodges, which it claims are the highest altitude lodges in the world (at 13,000-15,000 ft.), along the Camino del Apu Ausangate (in the Vilcanota range). Trek prices start at $795 per person.

By going off the standard trekking grid, when you get back to Cuzco you can be sure that not everyone in the coffeehouse will have the same bragging rights.

Machu Picchu Striking Facts

- ❖ It has been more than 100 years since the discovery of Machu Picchu in Peru. On July 24, 1911, Hiram Bingham III, a Yale professor, came to the vine-covered ruins of the ancient Inca city, so here is a bit of history of the country site and the players.

- ❖ It is unclear how these huge stones were moved to Machu Picchu or know how to cut stonecutters with precision. This is part of the wonder.

- ❖ Many times while you are looking around Machu Picchu, Llamas sometimes appear as if from nowhere.

- ❖ The design of Machu Picchu is highly organized. Its agricultural areas, top and bottom, are separated from urban areas, divided into East and West on the walls.

- ❖ The rainy season may cause some problems. Machu Picchu was closed in early 2010 for two months due to the heavy rains that wash the railroad tracks.

- The only time you will find small crowds in Machu Picchu is during the rainy season.

- 84. Many of the structures of Machu Picchu had a religious significance or importance of agriculture.

- About 1,000 people lived in the complex before it was abandoned, perhaps around 1572.

- Machu Picchu was built by Pachacuti ("He who shakes the earth"), the ruler of the Inca Empire, between two peaks - Machu Picchu and Huayna Picchu.

- Hiram Bingham father and grandfather were missionaries.

- Some say that Hiram Bingham was the model for Indiana Jones, the adventurous movie Fame.

- A decade after Hiram Bingham expedition to Peru was elected vice-governor of Connecticut. However, he had more in mind.

- Hiram Bingham III brought more than 5,000 artifacts from Peru on an expedition funded by the National Geographic and Yale University.

- It is unclear why Machu Picchu was abandoned, but some say it may be because water was scarce. However, this seems unlikely, given the focus on engineering and hydrology at the site,

Machu Picchu & Amazon River

as evidenced in part by the irrigation system. Others blame the Spanish conquest.

- ❖ Machu Picchu was abandoned in the 16th century.

- ❖ Nobody knows for sure exactly when Machu Picchu was built, but the best estimates suggest it was around the mid 15th century.

- ❖ Early explorers, led by Hiram Bingham, were unclear about the purpose of Machu Picchu. Remains found at the scene reportedly were all women, leading some to believe it was the temple of the virgins of the sun.

- ❖ If the Spanish did not find Machu Picchu, perhaps because they were distracted by his desire for the spoils of war, which is partly what led to disagreements between Diego de Almagro and Francisco Pizarro and Hernando.

- ❖ Where there once was an Inca empire, was then a Spanish empire that lasted 300 years.

- ❖ And what really could be? This is what Hiram Bingham wrote in Harper's Monthly in 1913 about coming to Machu Picchu. "... Suddenly we're in the middle of a jungle-covered walls of the maze of small and large, the ruins of buildings constructed with blocks of white granite, very carefully cut and well fitted without cement."

- Hiram Bingham thought he had found Vilcabamba, the "Lost City of the Incas" true, saying that was where the Incas took refuge from the Spanish.

- Hiram Bingham could not have been the first European to see Machu Picchu. Some say it was a German named Augusto Berns who met in 1867.

- Hiram Bingham did not really discover Machu Picchu, the residents knew was there, and a local Quechua-speaking guide, Melchor Arteaga, is said to have brought him there.

- Machu Picchu was, as expected, a UNESCO World Heritage Site in 1983.

- When you enter Machu Picchu, you will see why she was named one of the best-preserved pre-Columbian ruins in the world.

- You can go to Machu Picchu to Cuzco and back in 1 day.

- Aguas Calientes, which has grown haphazardly, as the crowds of tourists, has grown, offering basic and luxurious accommodation here at the starting point for the ascent to the Inca citadel.

- Depending on the level of luxury you want, your train ride to Machu Picchu can cost as lit-

Machu Picchu & Amazon River

tle as 100 dollars or up to 650 dollars to ride the Vistadome (Hiram Bingham)

- ❖ Cuzco, with a population of about 300,000 inhabitants, is the gateway to Machu Picchu that is 35 mi away.

- ❖ Symptoms of altitude sickness do not usually occur until the 8000 meters and Machu Picchu is located at 7,100 feet, but just in case, cut yourself some slack.

- ❖ To help deal with the altitude, make sure you drink plenty of water and avoid alcohol consumption.

- ❖ Some hotels provide oxygen to the visitors, while others offer coca tea, and it is not unusual to find packets of coca leaves for sale. Do not be afraid to chew them as they help alleviate the problems of altitude.

- ❖ At 11,150 feet, Cuzco requires acclimatization. Cuzco means "navel" or "center" of the earth. Without a doubt, was the center of the Inca civilization.

- ❖ Since the Incas had no written language system, the original spellings of the words are highly variable. The word Inca, for example, writes about Inca Ygna or Inga.

- ❖ About half of Peru's population is Quechua, a South American group with their own native language and spoken by the Incas.

- ❖ Peru borders with five countries: Ecuador, Brazil, Bolivia, Chile and Colombia.

- ❖ At 496,218 square miles, Peru in western South America, is about the size of the three Californias, However, Peru has a smaller population.

I hope that you have enjoyed very much the highlands of the Amazon jungle in the ancient ruins of Machu Picchu. Now is time to head down the Andean mountains until we reach the Amazonian flatlands to navigate the Amazon river.

> *"Despite all the challenges offered by the Inca trail, you'll be set for a wonderful experience which keeps trekkers coming back, year after year. It'll be a decision that you'll never regret! Welcome to Machu Picchu!" --by Gretel Morera*

Machu Picchu & Amazon River

HEADING TO THE AMAZON

The Most Beautiful Journey on Earth

Navegating the Amazon river is a dream of millions of people from around the world.

Obviously, there are still many people who relate the Amazon with nightmares and wild adventures full of adrenaline. They imagine the piranhas, anacondas, and other species unknown to us. They have heard stories about weird frogs with unicorn appendages. They have heard reports on the news about insects and wildlife never discovered until now; ones that stun the scientists. However, modern advances in technology have brought the Amazon closer to you, and the days connecting the Amazon trips to horror movies have been left behind.

Traveling is easy and now from anywhere you can conveniently catch a flight and spend a couple of days in the Amazon rainforest. You could make a longer journey, discover that the Amazon is full of brilliant and magical moments, and always make you feel grateful for given yourself the opportunity to enjoy this natural wonder.

Because it is so easy, safe, and fantastic to visit and

Machu Picchu & Amazon River

navigate the biggest river in the planet, all sorts of extraordinary feats has being accomplished.

In April 2007, Mr. Martin Strel, at the age of 53, became the first person to swim the entire Amazon River. This tells you that it is perfectly fine to be in the water, even though people will tell you their versions of the dangers that lurk below the surface. Mr. Strel swam the world record-breaking distance of 3,273 miles, which is longer than the width of the Atlantic Ocean.

On your journey, you will not have to stay in the boat all the time. When the temperature is too hot, take a dip in the refreshing waters of the Amazon and do so without the fear of being eaten slowly and painfully by piranhas.

If you're still thinking that it is dangerous to visit the Amazon, ask Mr. Ed Stafford, a retired British Officer, who walked the complete length of the Amazon River in 868 days, a world first. After walking through the Peruvian and Colombian portions of the riverbanks, In August 2010 he entered the Brazilian Atlantic ocean, the end of the Amazon river. His only complaint has been the mosquitoes, during the one time that he ran out of repellent.

You Can Surf in the Amazon

Allow me also to mention that there is surfing in the Amazon. During certain seasons, usually around January and February, you will find the most passionate surfers, riding the "Pororoca." This is a wave of up to 5 meters high, ranging up to 700 miles inland upstream.

One world record, related to the Amazon, is for surfing. Mr. Picuruta, a surfer from Brazil, rode the wave for more than 37 minutes, covering a distance of more than 7.8 miles in the presence of an official Guinness judge.

Golfers Do Have a Few Precautions

You can also play golf in the Amazon, at the only club that will deliver a machete when you start your first round. This field is a difficult adventure of nine par 5s. As you can imagine, birdies and eagles are not as important as watching for snakes hidden off the fairways, alligators in the bunkers, or piranhas lurking in the wells. Additionally, please try to avoid the anacondas.

There is much more about this unbelievable river, and I guarantee that you are going to be delighted. Stop making excuses, buy some mosquito repellent, and bring along your swimming trunks; because, when the heat gets tough, we will jump in together with the Amazonians, young and old, and do a historical swim in the grand Amazon.

Now that's something to write home about, especially since your friends won't know that the piranhas aren't a danger unless you have an open wound.

So let's start our trip full of confidence. You will be just fine, and, before you realize it, you will be back home and or back at your office, going through your normal, everyday routine.

Today, the Amazon is available to all, and I promise that if you follow the recommendations in this book, you will be able to observe anacondas, piranhas, and other great and unique species that will make your trip an experience you will remember until the last days of your life.

What I Want For You

After eradicating the fears and myths that I had about Machu Picchu and Amazon basin, I noticed the relief of stress that results once I had the right information. This was precisely the initial motivation for writing this book. Far from being a travel guide, this is an invitation for you to realize your dream of visiting Machu Picchu and navigating the Amazon sooner than you think by taking advantage of my experiences.

Let me show you how to do it safely, conveniently, and inexpensively. While you are reading this book, imagine that you are there in the Amazon, talking to the local people, dancing the salsa on the riverboat, and boarding the plane. Taking an imaginary adventure in your mind is the first step to actually making it a reality.

Nevertheless, the travel experience that I am proposing is not simply for you to entertain yourself and enjoy the scenic beauty that this powerful river offers, but an invitation to come on a journey that will make a positive difference in your life, as it did in mine.

I wish you became more aware of the world's environmental problems, the preservation of our invaluable natural resources, our global warming issues and the current deforestation in the Amazon.

Amazon Striking Facts

- ❖ The "mightiest of the giant rivers", the Amazon River is 4,250 miles in length. Just few miles longer than the 4,184 miles that makes up the Nile River in Africa. The Amazon River also has the biggest debit of all rivers.

- ❖ In 2001, the National Geographic Society found that the Nevado Mismi, located in the Peruvian Andes, was the source of water for the Amazon River. The Amazon's debit, at 200,000 cubic meters/second is 60 times larger than the Nile's: and, most importantly, because it delivers more than 20% of the freshwater volume that makes its way into the oceans, it is of great value.

- ❖ In one second, the Amazon pours more than 55 million gallons, or 600,000 cubic meters of water, into the Atlantic Ocean, which dilutes the ocean's saltiness for more than 100 miles from the shore.

- ❖ The river rises in a glacial lake in the Peruvian Andes, at 18,363 ft above sea level and only 100 miles off the Pacific coast. The locals call this stretch of the river Apurimac, while some locals in Brazil call it Solimões. It extends from the Andes Mountains in Peru, through Colombia, and then to the Atlantic Ocean in Brazil.

- ❖ The Amazon has more than 1,100 tributaries along its course, some very powerful. The volume of the Amazon is the same as the Mississippi River, the Nile, and the Yangtze rivers combined, forming a layer of fresh water for more than 100 miles into the Atlantic.

- ❖ The river enjoys summers in both hemispheres, and their water levels vary greatly; because of the rains, the oscillation can reach more than 12 meters.

- ❖ Each year, the Amazon River brings tons of solid particles deposited at its mouth, giving food for fish. It is responsible for the creation of the world's largest river island, Marajo Island, which is approximately the size of Switzerland.

- ❖ The Amazon is the widest river in the world. Its starting width is 300 miles, and yet, many miles from its mouth, the Amazon River can be as wide as 25 miles in the wet season. This means that in some places you can't see the banks from the one side to the other.

Machu Picchu & Amazon River

- ❖ At its mouth in the Atlantic, it widens to as much as 200 to 320 miles, depending on the season. Furthermore, every year, it widens up to 2 meters due to the waves breaking the banks.

- ❖ The river is also very deep and can reach depths up to 130 meters in some places, making it possible for marine vessels to travel up to 2,400 miles inland.

- ❖ The Amazon River flows through the center of the forest and feeds more than two thirds of all fresh water sources found on earth. It also has more than 22,000 miles of waterways and several million more miles navigable by canoe through swamps and forests.

- ❖ There are more than 3,000 fish species that have been identified; this is more species than throughout the Atlantic Ocean.

- ❖ The Amazon is the mightiest and most bioactive natural phenomenon on the planet. It is described as the "lungs of our planet" because it provides the global environment of essential services, such as recycling carbon dioxide into oxygen. It is estimated that more than 20% of the Earth's oxygen is produced in the basin of this river.

- ❖ The Amazon is home to many animals, especially "extreme" creatures, like catfish, which weigh up to 40 lbs in the US. However, in Brazil, they have been found to weigh more than 200 lbs.

- ❖ There are also the anacondas and pirarucu fish (the largest of its kind) and, of course, the piranha, which are perhaps the most ferocious animal on the planet.

I could go on and on mentioning all the world records that are attributed to this giant river, but, as mighty as it is, at the same time is very fragile and gentle.

In addition and even with all the weird creatures living in its water, with proper guidance, it is completely safe and stress free to navigate the Amazon.

Believe me; this sea of water will reward you with fantastic sights and unforgettable experiences.

It is such a vivid experience that a visit to the river should be in everyone's list of places to see.

Machu Picchu & Amazon River

Please help protect and conserve the environment   101.

MYNOR SCHULT

THE BEST JOURNEY OF YOUR LIFE

AS you already know experienced in Machu Picchu Latin America is a magical land, with breathtaking mountains scenery and home of the world's largest river.

In this chapter, you will become familiar with the details related to navigation on the river, whether you decide to make it a complete journey, from beginning to end, or simply travel to one country or even to just one city. Whichever way you choose, it will be a beautiful experience. Additionally, you will find a brief description of the journey and everything you need for planning your own trip.

In the following chapters, you can read more details for each of the three sectors into which we have divided the journey.

In the Western Sector, the main topic of this book, we travel from the plains at the base of the Peruvian Andes downstream to Colombia. It is here that the river forms the triple frontier between the countries of Peru, Colombia, and Brazil.

Machu Picchu & Amazon River

Then, in the Central Sector, described in more details in the book "AMAZON RIVER: COLOMBIA" we will sail from Colombia to Brazil, more specifically from the city of Leticia in the state of Amazonas, Colombia, to the city of Manaus (Amazonas' state capital) in Brazil.

Finally, the last sector, the Eastern Sector, is covered in "AMAZON RIVER: BRAZIL". It describes the journey from Manaus, one of the most remote cities in Brazil, navigating through the town of Santarem, and, finally, all the way to the end in the city of Belem at the Atlantic Ocean.

In "AMAZON RIVER: THE WILD ROUTES" you will be able to obtain details of the bus trip from Caracas, capital of the Republic of Venezuela, to the city of Manaus. At this time, this is the only land access connecting this jungle city.

Additionally, these wild routes are only recommended for enthusiastic hard-core adventurers. These routes will require more preparation because you have to travel through mountains and forests for hundreds of miles just to reach a gateway city in any of three sectors mentioned above. Just the journey to cities, like Iquitos or Manaus, is an adventure by itself. What is included here are routes coming from deep within the Peruvian Andes Mountains, as well as routes into the Amazon River from Ecuador, specifically from the city of Coca.

Europeans who want to take advantage of their

transatlantic flight can also find value here. The two best routes to visit the Amazon River have been included. The British who are coming to visit Georgetown in British Guyana prefer this first route; from here, they can visit the city of Manaus.

The last route is a trip for French people, who usually fly directly from Paris to Cayenne, French Guiana. From here, they can visit the Brazilian states of Amapá and Pará, in the most northern coast of Brazil, to enjoy a visit to see the wide mouth of the Amazon River meeting the Atlantic Ocean.

All these routes are included in my bestseller book "Amazon the River For the First Time… and Forever." Available for sale in all major bookstores including B&N and Amazon.com

Please keep in mind that even though this is not an "expedition" to the Amazon, obviously, it still requires a bit more preparation than a weekend city getaway. For example, you must have your Yellow Fever vaccination with the respective certificate to take along to show to border authorities when required.

On the other hand, if you travel to the gateway cities recommended in this book, the preparations for your trip are minimal. These towns, although they are in the middle of the jungle, are equipped with everything that you might need, including doctors, hospitals, pharmacies, supermarkets, clothing stores, souvenir shops, opticians, liquor stores, restaurants, bars, clubs,

Internet services, international calling, and mobile services, and all types of transport services, including airports, and much more.

In fact, the smallest city gateway is Leticia. Combined with the population of its neighbor towns in Brazil and Peru, this area has more than 100,000 inhabitants, plus a good amount of daily visitors from neighborhood villages and tribes that come to shop and sell their products in this tri-border area.

The Amazon Lifestyle

Before starting the journey, you must understand that the lifestyle in the Amazon is very simple in every way, so the opportunities to wear your Armani suit are slim to none. In addition, I can guarantee that you will end up using only half of the clothes that you are taking with you.

The weather in this part of the world is hot and humid throughout the year. Everybody dresses casually all the time, so, after a couple of days in the Amazon, you'll realize that nobody pays attention to your jewelry or any of your fancy accessories. Nobody even cares if you are wearing the same clothes that you wore yesterday.

For that reason, I guarantee that it will not be long before you adapt to local customs, so you will most likely end up using your shorts and your favorite T-shirt the whole time. You will also develop an unfailing friendship with your sandals.

The best advice that I can give you is to travel very light. Then you will have the opportunity to buy some local items that can be used not only during your stay in the jungle, but also take them home, impregnated with fabulous memories.

Honestly, the only items that you must bring with you are your camera to take pictures, your personal medications, your vaccinations, and your passport with the required visas. Everything else could be purchased locally, especially in case you forget something. The most important thing to bring with you is an attitude of discovery and appreciation for the opportunity to be in one of the most coveted destinations in the world.

Where Will You Start?

If you decide to start your journey in Lima or Cuzco Peru, upon arrival you will take an hour and a half local flight to reach the jungle city of Iquitos, in the state of Loreto in the Peruvian Amazon.

If you decide on Colombia, upon arrival to Bogota, you must take another domestic flight. Two hours later, you will be landing in the city of Leticia, a city founded on the banks of the Amazon River.

It is important to realize that once you reach the Amazon basin, there are no roads to travel within the area. The waterways are the only form of transportation, except for occasional charter flights.

Are you ready? Then Let us start this unforgettable journey right here where the Amazon begins.

> *"Pollution, overfishing and overuse have put many of our unique rivers at risk. Their disappearance would destroy the habitat of countless species. It would unravel the web of marine life that holds the potential for new chemicals, new medicines, unlocking new mysteries. It would have a devastating effect on communities from the Amazon to USA -- communities whose livelihood depends upon the rain forest. " Former US President Bill Clinton*

"FOR THE AMAZON RIVER, THERE MUST BE A BEGINNING"

The Beginning Was Controversial

Now there are two schools of thought about the birth of the world's longest and biggest river.

For years, people said that the Amazon was born in an indigenous community called Comunidad Grau, closed to the small City of Nauta, about 35 miles from the city of Iquitos in the Peruvian Amazon.

Mynor Visiting Comunidad Grau

However, a National Geographic expedition certified that the uninterrupted flow of water that forms the Amazon River is born high in the Andes Mountains, of-

Machu Picchu & Amazon River

ficially giving the Amazon River a total length of 4,250 miles.

In 1971, a National Geographic expedition, led by Explorer and Journalist Loren McIntyre, identified Nevado Mismi as the source. That conclusion has been the reason for changing the National Geographic maps of the region ever since. Without precise instruments, verification has proved elusive, and it is the subject of argument and speculation.

The source of the Amazon River was finally pinpointed by a five-nation National Geographic expedition, using state-of-the-art Global Positioning System (GPS) navigational gear. Ned Strong of Lexington, Massachusetts, led four reconnaissance trips in 1998 and 1999. Another team member, Piotr Chmielinski, was the first person to navigate the entire length of the Amazon in 1991.

The point of origin of the mighty Amazon River is a trickle of water coming off a cliff high on a slope of the Nevado Mismi, an 18,363-foot high mountain in southern Peru.

The person in charge of the instruments that nailed it was Geographer Andrew Johnston of the Smithsonian Institution's National Air and Space Museum in Washington. The source of the river, he says, can be defined as the most distant point in the drainage basin from which water runs year-round, or the furthest point from which water could possibly flow into the ocean. The "Nevado Mismi fits both these definitions."

The team consisted of 22 people representing the United States, Peru, Canada, Spain, and Poland. They explored all five of the remote Andean rivers that combine to form the Amazon: the Apurimac, Huallaga, Mantaro, Maranion, and Urubamba-Vilcanota.

Traveling by foot, jeep, bicycle, and horseback, the expedition worked from a base station near the confluence of several tributaries of the Apurimac River. They used GPS gear to map the path of the Continental Divide, the boundary of the Amazon River drainage basin, and to map the area's drainage features. Their instruments were accurate within a range of 1-5 meters (3-6 feet).

However, in this book we will start our journey in Nauta, Peru, where the Maranon and Ucayali rivers unite their waters. The only reason we begin our journey here is for the convenience of travel, since west of the city of Iquitos, the routes are extremely difficult for the ordinary tourist. In fact, these western routes are covered in more detail in my book "Amazon River The Wild Routes".

For ease of planning your trip, we will divide the river into three separate areas as follows:

Machu Picchu & Amazon River

Sector Divisions

Sector	Origin	Destination
WESTERN	IQUITOS, Loreto, Perú	LETICIA, Amazonas, Colombia
CENTRAL	LETICIA, Amazonas, Colombia	MANAOS, Amazonas, Brazil
EASTERN	MANAUS, AM, Brazil	BELEN, Para, Brazil

According to my travel experiences along the river, although the first sector is the smallest of the three, the western section is the most rewarding because of the large number and variety of flora and fauna.

Also, this sector will detail the trip from Iquitos, continuing downstream for amazing scenery, until we reach the village of Santa Rosa, one of the last villages in the Peruvian Amazon River, which is opposite the city of Leticia, Colombia.

This city borders the small town of Tabatinga, Brazil, forming the area better known as the Triple Frontier. It is at this precise point where the river joins the three bordering countries Peru, Colombia, and Brazil.

Have you already made a decision about which sector of the river you will enjoy while visiting the Amazon? Do you want to taste the fabulous seafood in Peru, while escaping to the ruins of Machu Picchu? Better yet, will you take salsa-dancing classes in Colombia, during the afternoon, and, in the evening, enjoy the rhythms of samba in Brazil? Alternatively, you may have been practicing Portuguese language skills, since you've already decided to embark on a 100% Brazilian adventure.

On the other hand, maybe you are one of those lucky travelers with lots of time, energy, and resources to travel the river from start to finish. Whatever your decision may be, keep reading for information that you will need to help you achieve your traveling goals with lots of fun.

In the following chapters, we will discover together how much money and time is needed to travel each of the segments. At the end of the book, I will also give details of the transportation company so that you can confirm pricing and schedules before you travel. However, you will notice that things change very little in the Amazon.

Furthermore, I will let you know any special considerations that you need to have, especially concerning your safety. However, I can give you a heads up: the Amazon is a very safe place in every way, whether you are in Peru, Colombia, and/or Brazil. You will probably feel much more secure than in most cities in the world.

To have a wonderful experience, all you need is to exercise the same cautions that you would in Madrid, Chicago, or Buenos Aires.

In addition, the boat ticket price includes meals on board and is a great opportunity to become familiar with the local cuisine. However, if you do not like rice, beans, or other foods enjoyed by the locals, do not worry. Onboard, there is a small store with sandwiches, cookies, sodas, cold beer, and other things favored by tourists. These can be purchased at very inexpensive rates. If you have unique food preferences, bring your own snacks and fruit for this short journey.

What sector is the best one to visit is always the big question. A question has equally viable and exciting answers and can be overwhelming for travelers to decide.

Finally, I share with you that the main question from my readers is what is the best sector to visit? Due to the impressive size of the river, it is overwhelming for most people to decide the best place to start their journey. This book will help to point you in the right direction

The Amazon Basin is Vast and Expansive

This book is only about how to navigate the Amazon River and does not refer to the entire Amazon basin, which has a presence in nine countries.

Secondly, I hope you enjoy the river from start to finish, an experience that will change your life forever. Because most travelers have a limited amount of time, usually no more than 10 to 20 days, I highly recommend the Western Sector from Iquitos, Peru, to Leticia, Colombia. (Or the other way around)

This part of the Amazon River is the least traveled by ships and boats, and it is where you have the best chance to see the best flora and wildlife of the Amazon.

In addition, more than 60, friendly, indigenous groups inhabit this area with the great majority being descendants of the Indian tribes of the Ticunas, Boras, Huitotos and other ethnicities.

Another great advantage of Western Sector is that you will cut travel time in half for the trip to Manaus from anywhere in the US, Canada, or Europe. The vast majority of these flights must have connections in San Paulo or Rio de Janeiro.

Instead of spending two additional days in travel, invest your time in the jungle. Another important advantage is that the cities of Iquitos in Peru and Leticia in Colombia have is that they are very affordable, compared to Manaus and Belem.

Finally, nowadays the exchange rate in Colombia and Peru are far more favorable than the local currency in Brazil.

Nevertheless, the main reason is that this area has access to some of the most impressive natural parks throughout the Amazonia.

From Iquitos, about 60 miles away, you could visit

the fantastic natural reserve of Pacaya-Samiria. From Tabatinga and only two hours deep into Brazilian territory, you will find the Natural Reserve of Palmira that will delight you with wild Amazon beauty. While you are in Leticia, it is practically mandatory to visit the National Park Amacayacu, 90 minutes away by fast boat transportation.

There you can experience a much closer encounter, not only with endemic plants and animals, but also with local tribes who handle the administration of this park.

Is Colombia Safe?

Because in this imaginary trip navigating the Amazons we are going to travel the western section that reaches from Iquitos in Peru all the way east to the Colombian border, let me address a question that may be a concern from you. Is Colombia safe?

Until recently, the political situation in Colombia was unstable, and the country as a whole was not recommended as a tourist destination. However, during the last 10 years, Colombia has greatly improved their social situation. After personally traveling to all major cities in Colombia, I can assure you that today is a safe destination.

In 2008, more than 1.8 million tourists visited Cartagena and San Andres, on the Atlantic coast, in addition to the Colombian Amazon. These destinations have always been far away from problem areas, and, today, they are even safer places.

The city of Leticia is only accessible by boat or plane, and it is protected by national armies from the three countries that form the triple border, alienating any illegal activity that may want to hit the area. Anti-social individuals have no place to run, except the jungle, a very unattractive hiding place for criminals.

After making several trips to the city of Leticia, I can assure you that there is virtually no crime in this city or its vicinity.

If we take into account the variety and quantity of animals, plants, and marine life, accessibility to many tribes, the ease and speed of access, and the great value that you get for your money, I highly recommend you visit this part of the Amazon. Whether you want to go upstream from Leticia to Iquitos or you slip downstream from Peru to Colombia, either way I guarantee you will be extremely satisfied.

Therefore, let us wait no longer and come with me to Iquitos, Peru, to start this historic journey, visiting this mystical giant named the Amazon River.

"The risk of coming to Colombia is falling in love with its landscape, its people, its cuisine, its fairs and festivities and its artisans and their colors. In reality, the only risk is wanting to stay." Proexport Colombia

Machu Picchu & Amazon River

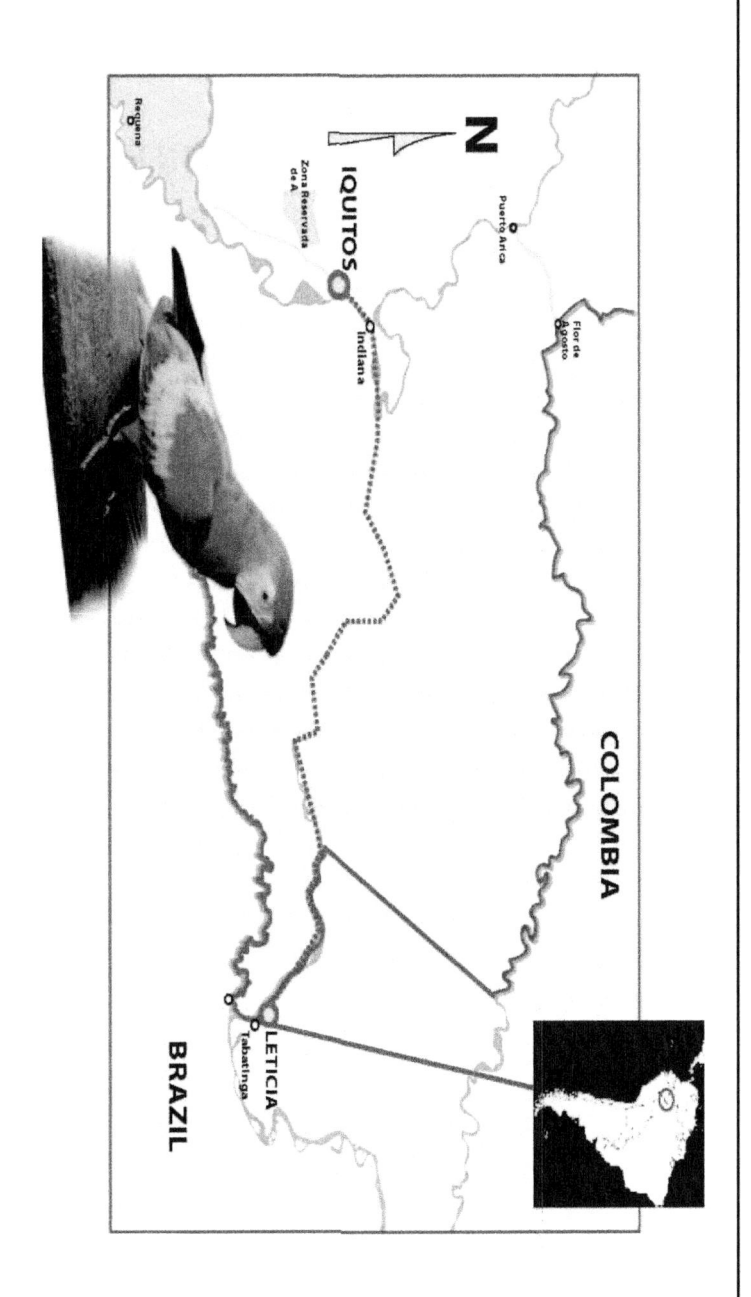

Please help protect and conserve the environment   117.

NAVIGATING REMOTE AMAZON WATERS

The magic of this Peruvian sector is that there is so much biodiversity here. While you're on this trip, at times, you will as if you have reached the end of the earth or taking a trip to Jurassic Park.

Don't worry, though, because it will not be long before you are brought back to reality by the thunderous noise of thousands of motorcycles if you happen to be in Iquitos. It is worth mentioning that, for city dwellers, the bustle of the city is always welcome after spending the first few days in the jungle, listening only to "strange noises", while amongst the plants.

This Western Sector does offer some convenience. You could begin your morning in bed just relaxing at your hotel; enjoy a steaming, delicious coffee in your Iquitos hotel connecting your computer to greet your online friends, while enjoying the comforts at a luxurious hotel. Just few hours later, you could be discovering one of the many natural reserves, such as Pacaya-Samiria, a place where you feel as if you've traveled back in time hundreds of years.

Machu Picchu & Amazon River

It is an understatement to say that Western Sector is one of the most gorgeous parts of the Amazon. The low and usually slow nautical traffic still allows you to see some of the most wild and striking wildlife without even getting off the boat.

Indigenous Tribes

In this sector, you will enjoy the span of the river and see some extensive parts that measure more than 10 mi from one side to another. At the same time, when the water level is low, you will be able to detect the unbelievable drop in water level where, at some points, the indigenous colonies look as if they are living several feet above your boat. The height difference when the river is full and when the river is its low point is about 35 to 40 feet. That's a lot and it's exciting as it is quite possible that your trip down the river, just few days later, could be vastly different from what you saw upstream.

Here you will have the best chances to admire pink dolphins, giant tortoises, and small turtles, such as the endemic Matamala, also known as the turtle of the Amazon. You can go fishing in search of giant Pirarucu, the largest fish of the Amazon, which can weigh over 400 kg or 880 pounds. Additionally, in Micos Island (Monkey Island), get ready to observe many types of primates that took this island as their own refuge few decades ago.

In the Natural Reserve of Pacaya-Samiria, you can spend time with a few tribes in the Amazon, without applying for any special permit to visit them. On the Brazilian side, only two hours by boat from Tabatinga, you can choose to visit and stay overnight in the Natural Reserve Palmari. Once in Palmari Reserve, safe tours can be arranged to go deeper into the jungle to visit some of the neighboring tribes, but I will give you more details about this Palmari Reserve in the next chapter.

The more common and colorful creatures of the rainforest, such as cockatoos, parrots, and papagallos are absolutely delightful here. Their colorful beauty has given even fame to this rainforest; it saturates the environment along with their tireless chattering and endless, harmonic songs.

If you like, exclusive flowers and unique plants, you will be amazed while admiring many. The floating Victoria Regia is the world's largest water lily with six feet round leaves and a beautiful white flower that only blooms during a full moon.

Wonderful Scenic Excursions

The most important characteristic of this sector is that it is wild. However, it is very convenient and very safe. From here, you can also make special trips to some of the most beautiful eco-hotels that you can imagine, but, usually, to reach them requires several hours of walking through the forest.

Machu Picchu & Amazon River

What you do need to know, in greater detail, is that to truly capture the beauty, the essence, and the sensational smells and colors of this enchanted forest, you may have to do a couple of short walks in either of the different national parks or the natural reserves.

As you travel through this vast sea of fresh water, whether you do it on a slow boat or a speedboat, remember to be vigilant in search of the elusive pink dolphins, giant tortoises, and other animals typical of this area. More importantly, alert your senses, and create unforgettable memories with the help of your camera and your notebook, but especially record them in your heart.

Remember, at all times, that most likely this is a once in a life journey; even though the Amazon is very special, it remains a remote place. Chances are, perhaps this will be your only visit. This perspective will prove very useful when the heat, mosquitoes, and other little things may be bothering you, while waiting for your already delayed ship to lift anchors.

Remember that this trip represents a unique privilege for you, because there is no guarantee that with the destructive power of our generation, there will be much left 30 years from now. So enjoy the beauty and the magic of the jungle while you can, and do not let the minor inconveniences pollute your beautiful vacation.

IQUITOS CITY

The city of Iquitos is surprisingly large, and the city of destination for foreigner that want to visit the jungle in Peru. For this imaginary Amazon trip, we will begin our journey in Iquitos until we reach Santa Rosa, the Peruvian village across the river from Leticia and Tabatinga.

The city of Iquitos is home to approximately half a million people in the middle of the Peruvian jungle. The city is very hot, with high humidity all year long.

Iquitos is located in the middle of nowhere, but it is full of fun activities for visitors. There are plenty of hotels in all categories, with comfortable and modern services, including business centers with wireless Internet and services for international calls.

In Iquitos, plenty of stores provide you with any item you may need to survive in the jungle or in the city. The restaurants, some of them of internationally acclaimed, can be found on almost every corner, along with pharmacies, bakeries, liquor stores, supermarkets, travel agencies, taxis, and buses to the nearby districts outside the city.

Iquitos has several different health centers and

two hospitals, one for civilians and one for the military. The military hospital inside the base of the Peruvian Navy could be used for major emergencies.

As part of a fun day, golfers can have a unique experience, playing their favorite sport in the middle of the Amazon. In this beautiful and challenging Iquitos nine-hole course, you will play in the midst of the waters of the Amazon and in a lush forest, which includes water wells with real piranhas and sand traps with an occasional alligator. So bring enough balls, because, if you are a poor golfer, you can become lunch for the anaconda.

At night, the businesses of the city decrease their rhythm, but other night activities, like dancing, dining, and walking along the river are common practices among locals and tourists. As with any other major city, it is necessary to exercise caution at night, especially if traveling alone. However, overall, this is still a very safe city, as most cities in the jungle.

A Bit of History Awaits

In late 1880, the "rubber boom" brought a great economic prosperity to the entire Amazon region until its decline in 1912. Still the legacy of the era of rubber can be seen in the architecture of elegant mansions imported from Portugal and other European cities. Moreover, if these mansions in the middle of the jungle do not impress you, then you probably will be surprised to find the engineer Eiffel's house. (Yes, this same Mr. Eiffel designed the Eiffel Tower in Paris.) The place is called The Iron House, and it is just one of many surprises waiting for you in the Amazon.

Unfortunately, for the locals, today, there is not much left from the "good old days" when the wealthy people of the city used to send precious mahogany wood from the jungle to Italy to be carved with exquisite designs by famous Italian artists. This carved wood was then returned back to Iquitos to be used in the construction of their mansions. I am sure, some of you will be surprised by the opulence in the midst of the jungle, but you will also be stunned by how hectic this jungle city is.

There are thousands of motorcycles, creating all kinds of sounds at very high decibels. In addition, Iquitos is one of the largest cities in the world that is not accessible by road; to get there; you must fly in or use the waterways that the Amazon River system has throughout Latin America.

To escape the noise from the mototaxis in Iquitos, take refuge in the local historical buildings, such as the Amazon Museum, built in 1863. The museum contains wonderful artwork and old photographs, belonging to the late nineteenth century, which enables you to view Iquitos in its glory days. Moreover, you must go to the Belem market and visit Pasaje Paquito. You must go with a local guide, who will explain how, for the last hundreds of years, the Amazon citizens have used local medicinal plants to cure any disease known to them.

The Shamans are Available to You

Personally, I have seen many times how their advice is sought even from distant lands, not just in America, but also from Europe. However, let me caution you. Lots of humility is needed to listen to these wise old men, sometimes with ragged looking clothes.

However, they are constantly sought out by scientists, mainly from major pharmaceutical companies in the world, who are always looking for the "miracle" cures that have been in possession of these Shamans for many centuries.

After a couple of days enjoying Iquitos, be prepared to leave this noisy town with its millions of horns and sirens and dive back in the jungle.

Nonetheless, before navigating the river to Colombia or Brazil, head west up, the river, to visit a couple of fascinating places on the outskirts of Iquitos.

One is the important and beautiful natural reserve of Pacaya-Samiria and the other is a visit to the indigenous community of Grau, the former birthplace of the Amazon River. Once you have completed these short trips upstream, then you will be ready to head downstream to the Colombia-Brazil border.

For now, let us navigate the Amazon River about 90 miles towards the Andes Mountains to find one of the most impressive reservations in the world.

Pacaya-Samiria

Not only is this the largest water reserve in Peru, but it is also one of the most important areas for the world because of its great biodiversity. The Peruvian government, since 1940, has protected the Pacaya-Samiria basin, formed by a couple rivers, and, still today, the reserve is only accessible by boat. It has an area of 5,139,680 hectares, equivalent to the size of New Jersey in the United States.

The reserve is shaped like a triangle, situated at the confluence of the Maranon and Ucayali. For many years, it was said to be the birthplace of the Amazon River, but now, thanks to the new satellite technology we know that those calculations were wrong.

The reserve has more than 80 lakes and about 50,000 people living on it, the majority of the Indians in villages are located along the edge of the reserve or around the lakes, and only a few live in the depths of the reservation. The average family consists of eight to ten people who live in houses made from materials found in the forest. Its main survival supplies consist of plantain, cassava, and fish (their basic diet).

The reserve is formed by three watersheds, including Samiria, Yanayacu, and Pacaya, and has several communities. The most accessible and visited are listed below.

Veinte de Enero – Observe the People

This is the entry point of the reserve and the most accessible with a human presence that is clearly strongly related to nature. , Remember that you're more than welcome, but please don't pollute. Be like them, follow their rules, and be peaceful with nature. Most notable in this indigenous community is that they conduct almost all their activities in a very sustainable way, using wisely, for centuries, local natural resources and reforestation.

Yarina – Haven for Photographers

An ideal place for a photographic expedition and bird watching, the Yarina territory has an area of "rescue of the environment", where different species are rescued from the grip of extinction. Its high level of biodiversity characterizes the area. Yarina tribes are also known for their expertise in the activities of sustainable resource exploitation.

Manco Capac – Fishing Resort

Manco Capac is the largest lake. This is the place where organized groups of fishermen practice sustainable living mainly eating fish like "Paiche", or pirarucu as it is known in Brazil. This lake offers an unforgettable view of the Amazon rainforest, giving also great opportunities for photography. However, you must follow the recommendations of natives, as the locals are officially responsible for overseeing any tourist activity. Don't get any ideas that you can hold any wild parties –

it's their turf!

Community of Grau – Lookout Point

Before leaving the city of Iquitos, I recommend visiting the community of Grau. Climb the 120 feet lookout structure for a panoramic view of the "old birthplace of the Amazon River. From the city of Iquitos, you can take a bus for less than a dollar or take a shared-taxi with air conditioning, which is quicker and will cost about $5 each way. The 60 mi distance will take approximately 75 minutes, via the only paved highway in thousands of miles.

Once in the small city of Nauta, you can take one of the local regular service boats to Community Grau, at a cost of $2 per trip, but note that the regular service is offered more frequently during the morning hours. If you arrive after noon, you may need to rent a private boat that will take you to Grau for less than $25 round trip.

As mentioned before, based on the National Geographic expedition of 1972 and today's modern satellite equipment, we now know that the Amazon originates closer to heaven, up in the Andes Mountains. The Nevado del Mismi is the place that was firmly established by the National Geographic expedition, as the source of the Amazon River, near 18,360 feet high and 100 mi west of Lake Titicaca, and nearly 250 mi southeast of Lima.

What is undeniable is the fantastic view brought by

the convergence of these two huge rivers. Each mighty on their own, the meeting of their water is as impressive as the Ucayali River from the Ecuadorian Andes. The Marañón River, as the locals call it, is the same Amazon River that comes from the Peruvian Andes.

After visiting the reserve and having done these short tours, begin your journey downstream to Colombia. During the tour, you will see many striking villages from the boat, or you could visit some of them located along the way. The most accessible and easiest to visit are closer to the cities of Iquitos and Leticia.

This is why it is more convenient to use these cities as a main base for traveling to these indigenous communities established along the Amazon's shore, as some of these indigenous communities may not have the tourist infrastructure necessary for your comfort.

In any case, read on to discover which of these communities have adequate infrastructure so that you and your family can enjoy your visits. Some of the main communities are listed below.

Pevas, Peru – Authentic Crafts

The small town of Pevas is the oldest European settlement in the Peruvian Amazon. When you visit this community, don't neglect to visit the neighboring indigenous communities of Bora and Huitoto, which are located just downstream. Here you can see how people live in these indigenous reservations and observe them in their flamboyant outfits, while they dance their traditional dances in a Maloka, which is the main home of any Indian reservation.

You also have the opportunity to view and purchase authentic crafts, including beautiful paintings of jungle scenes made in bark cloth, handbags, jewelry, fabrics of all types, and hammocks. Respect their traditions and purchase these items directly from the indigenous people whenever possible, as this simple gesture helps their communities and keeps them faithful to their traditions.

Caballo Cocha, Peru – Piranha Fishing

The city's name is a combination of Spanish and Quechua, meaning "horse of the lake." It has an approximate population of 4,223 inhabitants, including the mission town on Lake Caballo Cocha.

Here, as in most lakes of the regions, you can take a trip to see the Victoria Regia and concurrently observe a population living in close harmony with the jungle environment. This is where you have the opportunity to go fishing for piranhas, since usually these fish are found in greater numbers near the dark-water lakes, such as Lake of Caballo Cocha.

Santa Rosa, Peru – Not Many Tourist

Of the three cities in the tri-border area, Santa Rosa has the least amount of tourist infrastructure with very primitive facilities lacking good hotels, restaurants and nightlife. It's recommend to overnight in Tabatinga, Brazil or Leticia, Colombia.

Getting To Iquitos

Iquitos By Air:

As in most cities in the jungle, usually, there are no roads leading to them. The two main cities in this sector, Iquitos and Leticia, are no exception. However, both have excellent air transportation.

The city of Iquitos can easily be reached from Lima, the capital city of Peru. Currently, several local airlines serve Iquitos; among them, STARPERU and LanPeru complete at least eight direct flights every day. Back in Iquitos there are even more flights and planes in route to Lima that may stop in Iquitos to refuel, picking up passengers at the same time. Well-trained pilots and professional crews that use modern and comfortable Boeing 737s, with a capacity for more than 150 passengers.

Let me remind you again that due to the popularity of these routes, the prices are quite affordable, around $100 for any air flight between Lima and Iquitos. During low season, it's possible to obtain a one-way ticket for less than $70.

Here's an important money-saving tip: If you purchase tickets for the Peruvian local flights in your hometown, whether the USA, Canada, or Europe, then you will most likely be paying about $300 extra for each segment. Therefore, my recommendation is that after buying your international air ticket, (you should not pay more than $500 from your home city in America, $700 from Europe, or $900 from Asia and Oceania), visit the local airline websites that are listed at the end of this book, and buy directly from those local airlines saving up to $500.

At the other end of Western Sector, the city of Leticia has two excellent local airlines with daily service from the capital city of Bogota. Keep in mind that from Bogota you can do all your international connections and all your local connections to any Colombian city, just in case you decide to escape to the beautiful Caribbean beaches of Cartagena or San Andres.

From the city of Tabatinga, Brazil, there is the possibility of booking air flights bound for Manaus.

Finally, across the river and on the other bank of the Amazon, is the town of Santa Rosa in Peru. Here, the only air services to be found are very irregular military flights that are not always commercially available. It is not wise to plan your journey using this service. Actually, Santa Rosa has no commercial airline service, so the only form of transportation available to residents of Santa Rosa is to navigate upriver to Iquitos, which seems to be the last frontier for the Peruvians.

River Transport

Once you arrive to Iquitos, the only transportation outside the city is through waterways. Mainly, you have two different types of boats to travel and enjoy the giant among giants – the Amazon River.

The most common option is to take the slow cargo ships. This is what most of the local population chooses, as they are less expensive. The second option is to take the speedboats. Generally, tourists prefer the faster, all exclusive passenger speedboats.

The cargo ships depart for travel frequently, at least four times a week; and, usually, they take two full days to travel the 260 mi that separate the cities of Iquitos and Leticia. Remember to add an extra day to the time spent onboard if you reverse the trip upstream. From the city of Leticia to Iquitos, the boat will navigate against strong Amazon River currents. The cost of the ticket is less than $25, and it includes a place to hang your hammock and meals on board.

Generally, locals, students, and people who really want to experience the Amazon prefer the cheap transport on cargo vessels. If you have the time to travel through this sector, then make one trip on the slow boat and take the return trip on the speedboat.

Here's an Alternate Plan

Another way to enjoy this area is to book your flight arrival in Bogota, Colombia, and the departure flight from Lima, Peru, or vice versa. If you use an air transport company that provides service to both cities, such as American Airlines, Continental Air, Delta, COPA, TACA, and other European companies, the difference in price should be minimal. (A good place to check for airfare is www.Expedia.com)

The preferred way for most tourists, who always seem in a hurry, is the speedboat that travels every day, connecting major communities between the cities of Iquitos and Leticia. The cost each way is around $70 per person; and, in only 10 hours, you arrive at your destination. The ticket price also includes a quick breakfast and a lunch served aboard. Onboard you will find playing the latest "Hollywood" blockbuster hit from China or Bombay.

Daily, only one speedboat travels in each direction, leaving very early in the morning to arrive in the afternoon at your destination. Generally, the departure time is 5:00 am with arrival time around 2:40 pm. At the end of this book, you will find websites with more information, so you can refresh the schedules before departing your hometown.

The boat will depart from the main port of Iquitos,

and a mototaxi, the normal mode of transportation in most Amazonian cities, will charge you couple of dollars to drop you off at the port. However, be aware that they drive like maniacs, but do not worry. After a couple of scares, you will safely arrive at your destination.

Two companies, Transtour and Golfhino, offer passenger boat service between Iquitos and the tri-border area. The two companies are very reliable and bring safe service every day, traveling in opposite directions. As an example, on Monday the Golfhino Company travels from Iquitos to Leticia when the ship spends the night in the tri-border area. The next day it reverses the trip upriver, while the other company, Transtour, runs the river downstream from Iquitos.

No Need to Fear Being Stranded

Every day, the two boats journey in opposite directions. This is encouraging to visitors that are a little skittish about being in a largely remote area. It's possible that the boat could break down or other mechanical failures could occur.

The fear is that you will be stranded. However, with boats journeying in opposite directions, you're always just a boat away from being rescued. Moreover, here's something else you should know – the riverboat business must go on for people to earn a living. Because of that, they will do everything possible to keep the boats operational and well-tuned machines.

These passenger boats travel quite fast and are very comfortable, with space for 15 to 20 passengers. They are captained by people of considerable experience, properly trained and authorized. Commonly, the captains and the rest of their crew are residents of the area, with an intrinsic knowledge and vast Amazon familiarity, wisdom accumulated over the years of having grown up on the River.

In general, these faster boats only stop at some indigenous communities to leave or pick up passengers, but occasionally make "pit stops" to leave parcels with stranded fishing boats.

Every ship that arrives is the event of the day in those communities. Consequently, all the villagers, most of them Indians, dressed in shirts and jeans, flock daily to the harbor to watch what is going on. Their interest is to know who came, who is leaving, and, above all, what new food supplies are arriving.

Therefore, this is a great opportunity to take photos of how the natives live. The best time is when the river is at its maximum level between June and October.

Machu Picchu & Amazon River

The Apex of 3 South American Countries

You'll reach your destination in Santa Rosa in Peru, in the tri-border area, about 10 hours later. Here you will be surprised by the large activity and the crowds of people that you will find, mostly at the other side of the river, along the coast of Colombia and Brazil.

During the day, the ports are filled with fishermen, traders, beggars, and other characters common to commercial ports. At night, restaurants and dance clubs in the three countries, but mainly in Colombia and Brazil, will come alive with loud Latin and Brazilian rhythms coming from restaurants and bars.

This is a real opportunity to learn to dance salsa and enjoy an all-night Latin party with tropical flavor. Do not worry if you're not very skilled in these dances, since it is having a good time that counts most.

To exit the small village of Santa Rosa, take a small boat that costs about a dollar to cross the river to the cities of Leticia in Colombia or to Tabatinga in Brazil.

These two small border towns are the international borders of two great countries separated only by a modest street called Avenida da Amizade (Friendship Avenue). Moreover, this is one of the few places on earth where you can visit three South American countries in less than one hour. How much fun it will be for you to have breakfast in Colombia, lunch in Peru, and dinner in Brazil without much travel time at all!

Leticia – You Have Arrived Colombia

Congratulations! You survived your first trip to the Amazon. We have arrived unharmed at the tri-border area, so Colombia and Brazil welcome you. I hope that this first trip on the river was not as scary as you were expecting and that your trip was honored by the presence of the mysterious pink dolphin as well as many more wildlife creatures.

In addition, I hope that your visit to Iquitos was more than what you expect from a city in the middle of the jungle. Now let's do the same in Leticia, Colombia. May I suggest that you take the time to locate the city of Leticia on a world map, because, when you find yourself dancing the salsa rhythms in a busy bar tonight, you will not believe that you are in the middle of the jungle.

Now let's visit the cities of Leticia in Colombia and Tabatinga, Brazil that together with the community of Santa Rosa in Peru form the tri-border area.

Machu Picchu & Amazon River

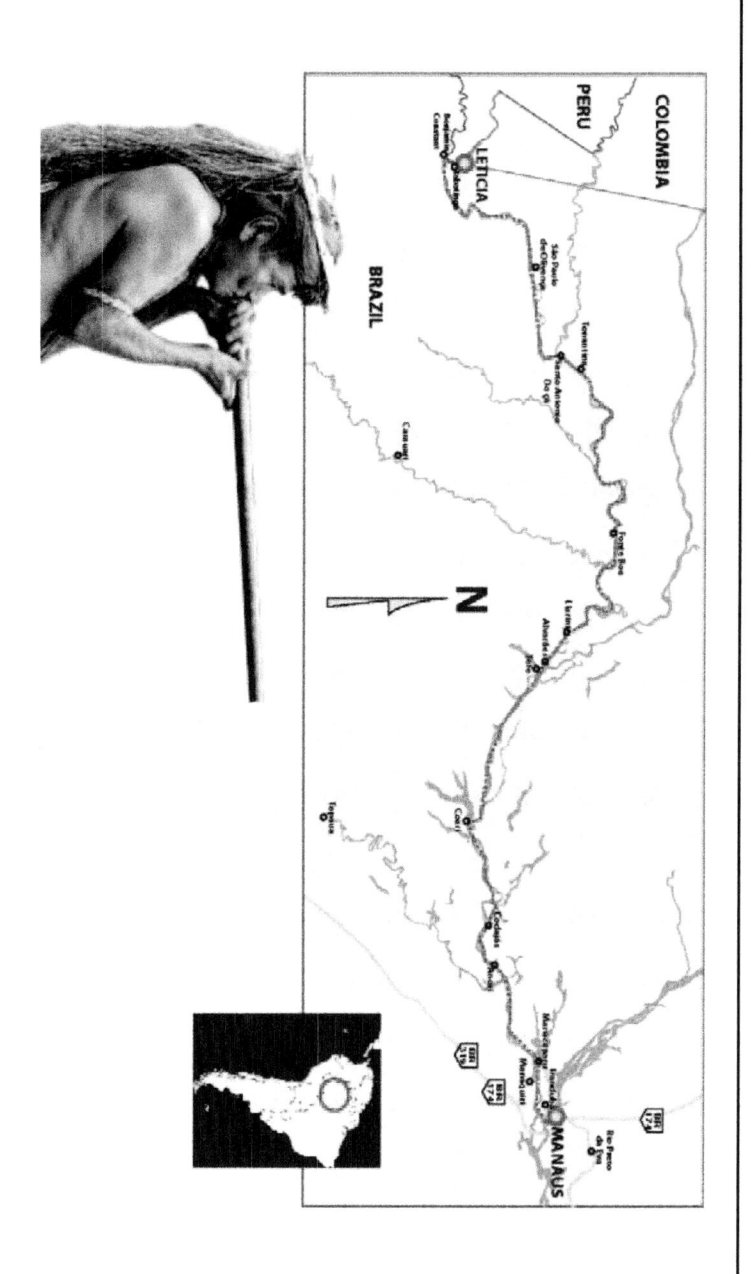

Please help protect and conserve the environment

Leticia, Colombia

If you are starting your trip here, the easiest way to reach the tri-border area is by air into the city of Leticia. It currently has at least three airlines serving the city with an excellent and economical service from Bogota, Colombia.

From Bogota, you can do all your international and domestic connections with any city in Colombia, especially in case you want to book a getaway to Cartagena or San Andres in the Colombian Caribbean. One airline is Satena, which belongs to the Colombian government. The other company, Aero Republica, is more reliable and is owned in part by Continental Airlines.

Aero Republica has connections to all Colombian cities and connections worldwide through its international hubs in Panama, Houston, and New York. Domestic flights from Bogota are very cheap, about $80 each way. The trips are very safe with modern aircraft and highly trained crews.

Please note that if you buy local flights in the U.S. or Europe, local fees can cost up to $600. Here's the solution: browse for your international ticket on one of your favorite travel sites, and then visit the websites of local airlines of Colombia, which appear at the end of the book and purchase your ticket directly with them.

This way you can save up to $500. It is also important that you consider that while Continental Airlines in the U.S. owns Aero Republica in Colombia, you still need to buy air tickets separately, in order to benefit with the savings on local fees.

Aero Republica Airlines

This airline operates Embraer 190 aircraft for 100 passengers, and it flies every day from Bogota, departing around 12:18 and arriving at 14:18 in Leticia. The return flight to Bogota Leticia leaves at 14:40 and takes a one-hour and 45-minute flight. In high season and during holidays, these companies tend to add more flights with up to four daily flights during the Christmas and Easter holidays.

Aires Airlines

AIRES is the second largest operator in the Colombian domestic market with a market share of 22% and daily flights to Leticia Amazonas with Boeings 737-700 aircrafts considered the best in the world for its features and reliability.

Air Satena

Air Satena operates Embraer 170 planes for 70 passengers, and it flies only on Mondays, Wednesdays, and Fridays. Departures are from Bogota to Leticia at 10:25 am, arriving at 12:15. The return flight to Bogota leaves at 12:45. (1 hour 45 minute flight)

Attractions in Leticia & Tri-Border Area

Although Tabatinga is larger in size and population, most activity occurs in the city of Leticia, since the city of Leticia has developed a modern infrastructure for trade and tourism comparable to any small town in Europe or America.

This is a very safe area for any tourist, and crime is practically nonexistent due to the presence of three national armies that protect their own borders. Perhaps because criminals have no hiding place except the jungle. Having been here many times, I assure you that this area is not only very beautiful but also safe. You will find friendly locals and quickly you will feel at home.

Cultural Events

Besides the common border represented by these two cities, they have created a wide range of art events, historical events, cultural events, social events, and natural events.

These towns offer urban infrastructure in the middle of the jungle, which serve visitor with all necessary services for trips into the forest or any service necessary to enjoy the city, including hotels, residences, traditional restaurants, agents, operators, craft shops, malls, bike rental service, currency exchange, banks, Internet services, and mobile communications. In fact, the city of Leticia has many taxis and minibuses that serve the entire area; the motorcycles are the primary means of transportation within cities, and there are enough points where you can rent them.

A key feature of this area is that many indigenous groups do not care about the borders imposed by whites. You will find families with the same cultures, customs, and lifestyles on both sides.

In fact, more than 26 ethnic groups still practice their own cultural practices and speak their own languages. The cultures are ancient ones, and, because of this, you have the opportunity to have an unforgettable experience, just by interacting with native communities, savoring their food and drinks, dancing their dances, and partaking in their rituals.

You could even accompany them on their walks through the jungle to perform their daily tasks, such as fishing, where they are still using artisan methods. Other additional opportunities are helping to create crafts, and, of course, you can even participate in shamanic experiences.

Leticia & Tabatinga – Outdoor Activities

The main attraction of this area is ecotourism; especially activities related to the great river, such as walking, swimming, observing wildlife, anthropology, exploring the river, fishing, jungle tours, and other outdoor activities. Nevertheless, there are several activities in the city of Leticia that you should attend such museums and parks.

Parks Santander - For Parrot Lovers

Enjoy the free concert every evening, with hundreds of parrots of different species belonging to this region. Do not miss this great eco-concert, which is incredibly loud, unique, and beautiful.

Leticia Serpentarium – For Snake Lovers

Observe and learn about different species of snakes in the Amazon here at Leticia Serpentarium. Many tourists love the tree house, where you can experience a night sleeping in the forest in a completely secure environment. The tree house even has a bathroom, and it is well protected against mosquitoes. The cost per night for two people is about $60, and I recommend that you make this one of your life experiences. Please find contact information at the end of the book.

Store Uirapuru – For Artifact Collectors

I usually do not make any recommendations for specific stores, but this place is a private museum and a souvenir store full of Indian artifacts, plants, and animals. Here you can admire the Matamala turtle, another Amazonian animal that hides away and lives its life in secret. This turtle is a small one, and the unique thing about it is that it has a unicorn, which seems prehistoric. Words won't describe it, so take 15 minutes and visit the shop. You can also see other fish, like piranhas, eels, and more. This is a great place to buy souvenirs, and your friends will love the authentic stuffed and dissected piranhas for less than $6. They will pack it and ship it to your office in New York or London, where you can constantly brag of your trip to the Amazon.

Local Markets – A 'Must Go' Place

The local market is always an obligatory visit for any tourist to the Amazon, as it is the main place to see neighbors come in different boats and canoes full of farm supplies, fish, livestock, medicinal plants, and many products unique to the region. At the market they sale, barter, or exchange with locals and tourists. Likewise, this is a good place to taste the most eccentric dishes of local gastronomy.

Benjamin Constant, Brazil

Benjamin Constant is 22 mi south of Tabatinga. It is the first stop where all boats leave from Manaus. From here, there is a road connection to Atalaya Do Norte, the entry point Palmari Nature Reserve. They also have fast boats, the "river taxi to Benjamin," leaving Tabatinga. It holds at least 10 passengers and the charge is $5 per trip.

Visit the Tribes in Palmari Reserve

What motivates most of the visitors to reach this remote area of the world? It is indeed the biological potential, the observation of nature, indigenous cultures, communities along the river, and the tranquility offered by Amazon, and the best place to find all these experiences is at Palmari Nature Reserve.

It is located in the Brazilian side, about 2 ½ hours from Leticia and Tabatinga by speedboat, or about 5 ½ hours by canoe. This place would be one of the most fun experiences in the Amazon, because you can arrange a very comfortable and safe visit to the indigenous tribes, such as Matiz, Marubos, and Mararunas.

Other fantastic and unique activities are learning to use real crossbows, hike or row into the jungle to spend a night in the jungle sleeping in a hammock, learning and experiencing the process to manufacture rubber, and more.

Of course, there are many more activities to do at this paradise, activities full of fun adventure and excitement, but we need to get on the boat that will take us down the river to Manaus navigating the 1000 mi from the Colombian border to the Capital of the Amazonas. As you may imagine, there are thousands of communities along the way before we get to the big city of Manaus, but the most important ones are Benjamin Constant, Sao Paulo Olivença, Amaturá, San Antonio de Iza, Tonantins, Jutai, Fonte Boa, Coari and Codajas.

Machu Picchu & Amazon River

There is no doubt that the tropical rainforests of the world are in danger. Every hour approximately six species of life in our tropical rainforests are destroyed. Experts agree that the number one cause of extinction in the tropical rainforest is due to the destruction of the tropical rainforest environment."

Jason Albright

Please help protect and conserve the environment

FROM MANAUS' JUNGLES TO BELEM'S BEACHES

This is the most popular sector of the river, and most people, when they decide to come to the Amazon, choose the city of Manaus. Usually, they fly into this huge city in the middle of the jungle and then take a boat down the river to the city of Belem, where the mouth of the Amazon is located right at the Atlantic Ocean.

Obviously, you can come back upstream in another boat, or take a flight back to Manaus; these two cosmopolitan cities have countless options and combinations of transportation to reach them.

However all details regarding this journey will be found on my book "Amazon River Brazil" or my bestseller "Amazon the River for the First Time… and Forever" on sale at all mayor book stores.

Machu Picchu & Amazon River

Please help protect and conserve the environment

CONSERVATION AND SUSTAINABLE TOURISM

The implementation of sustainable tourism in a responsible manner is perhaps one of the best ways to preserve the rainforest, and their biological and ethnic diversity while also helping to eradicate poverty. Ultimately, this contributes to the preservation of humanity.

No doubt, we all need to understand the value and monumental importance of the Amazon River for the preservation of humanity and unless we all practice sustainable tourism, it will be very difficult for future generations to come to enjoy this wonderful river, which undoubtedly is a lung for the entire planet Earth.

In addition, I confess that while writing this book, I am dreaming of tourism that is organized, efficient and green for our future generations. Sustainable tourism cannot be just a buzzword in the XXI century. After you visit the Amazon and return to your city, I hope that you will become, at least passively, an advocate to not only this natural wonder called the Amazon River but also an advocate of the natural resources of your own locality.

Until now, the concept of sustainable tourism may have been a very abstract concept for you but after visiting the Amazon, I assure you that you will understand exactly the practical applications of "sustainable tourism". You will be able to implement life lessons that you have learned on this beautiful journey.

A Prerequisite for Traveling

Throughout this book, I have been inviting you to navigate the river, but perhaps I forgot to tell you that there is only one prerequisite. That prerequisite is to implement this type of tourism, not only in learning and having fun in this so spectacular place, but by also contributing as a responsible tourist, respecting nature, not contaminating it, protecting it, and making practical use of all the recommendations that the indigenous peoples give you in the places that you visit.

Your contribution can be, for example, to put trash in the appropriate deposits. It can be that you do not burn, do not kill or remove the various species, both flora and fauna. It can be that you respect indigenous customs of the place.

Your Oxygen Source

I am frequently called and asked to encourage visitors to participate in local programs, either directly by giving support to any group of volunteers. It might be during your visit, or later when you go home, supporting different organizations, which today are actively taking care of our planet to try to ensure the survival of our own generation and generations to come. Above all, one of the main reasons this book is here is to remind you that we must not forget that the Amazon is the lungs of the world. The Amazon is responsible, in a large way, for the oxygen we breathe in California, China and Canada.

I know that in these days of global crisis, perhaps it might be difficult for you to visit the Amazon. However, I want to make sure, that I am making a conscious effort to transmit the sense of urgency that we should all give to the problems of global warming, deforestation and other environmental problems that are threatening our survival. Therefore, if, at this moment, all you would do is a small donation to support a community or other Amazonian entity of your liking, do it now, for a little help today may be vital to our future.

Even more important than any gift, is to implement sustainable tourism even in your own home. We all need to ensure better use of water, electricity, and better care of plants and trees around us. Just as we do when we travel, we consistently recycle waste from our homes or even better, minimize them.

Anyway, start planning your trip, because I know with certainty that unless it's in your heart to experience the exquisiteness of this beautiful uncrowded place, you may not understand the globalism of our problems.

Believe me, it is wonderful to feel the embrace of an

indigenous child and see the love that these people have for visitors. Amazingly, the Amazon people are friendly, humble, and loving. They see their way of life in peace with nature, fully integrated into it, living in harmony as though it's the only way to live.

You are Loved from the Minute They Set Eyes on You

"The knowledge we can gain from studying the Amazonian dark earths, found throughout the Amazon River region, not only teaches us how to restore degraded soils, triple crop yields and support a wide array of crops in regions with agriculturally poor soils, but also can lead to technologies to sequester carbon in soil and prevent critical changes in world climate." Johannes Lehmann

The best part is that they always welcome tourists warmly, despite the fact that many of us do not show any respect for their culture and its resources. (By cutting thousands of trees every day, we continue to endanger their survival, and, in the near future, we endanger our very own.) Indeed, recall that we are not only fighting for the conservation of natural resources,

I am also aware that I alone cannot eradicate poverty along the mighty Amazon River, but I know perfectly well that if, through this book, you become more conscious and firmly commit yourself to look after the precious resources that we still have, that would be more than enough.

My greatest wish is that you also decide to take concrete actions, eventually making a big difference in the lives of others. In this way, your friends may decide to imitate you,

but also for the thousands of people living in the Amazon for centuries.

Will You Embrace These Goals?

Similarly, I hope I conveyed that the preservation of the environment and the alleviation of poverty have become major goals in my life, because I believe these are essential to world peace and are a moral obligation for all of us who can do something about it.

I am also aware that I alone cannot eradicate poverty along the mighty Amazon River, but I know perfectly well that if, through this book, you become more conscious and firmly commit yourself to look after the precious resources that we still have, that would be more than enough.

My greatest wish is that you also decide to take concrete actions, eventually making a big difference in the lives of others. In this way, your friends may decide to imitate you, and, before you know it, you have formed a small group to help improve a community. As time goes by, a few years later the benefits will be pass on to others. And who knows… mainly along the way you help to the survival or a community.

May be in a couple of decades, your grandchildren that come to visit and enjoy the Amazon basin find it cleaner, greener, and different in many ways, all for the better.

To conclude, this important and essential chapter, I want to share with you some advice based on the Code of Ethics for Tourism of the World Tourism Organization (WTO). Pay close attention to Advice #1, which is directly related to our next chapter, about Indigenous Cultures.

The Responsible Tourist and Traveler

Travel and tourism should be planned and practiced as a means of individual and collective fulfillment. When practiced with an open mind, it is an irreplaceable factor of self-education, mutual tolerance and for learning about the legitimate differences between peoples and cultures and their diversity.

Everyone has a role to play creating responsible travel and tourism; governments, business and communities must do all they can, but as a guest, you can support this in many ways to make a difference:

1. Open your mind to other cultures and traditions – it will transform your experience, you will earn the respect of the local and always will be welcome. Be tolerant and respect diversity – observe social and cultural traditions and practices.

2. Respect human rights. Exploitation in any form conflicts with the fundamental aims of tourism.

Machu Picchu & Amazon River

The sexual exploitation of children is a crime punishable in the destination or at the offender's home country.

3. Help preserve natural environments. Protect wildlife and habitats and do not purchase products made from endangered plants or animals.
4. Respect cultural resources. Activities should be conducted with respect for the artistic, archaeological and cultural heritage.
5. Your trip can contribute to economic and social development. Purchase local handicrafts and products to support the local economy using the principles of fair trade. Bargaining for goods should reflect an understanding of a fair wage.
6. Inform yourself about the destination's current health situation and access to emergency and consular services prior to departure and be assured that your health and personal security will not be compromised. Make sure that your specific requirements (diet, accessibility, medical care) can be fulfilled before you decide to travel this destination.
7. Learn as much as possible about your destination and take time to understand the customs, norms and traditions. Avoid behavior that could offend the local population.

8   Familiarize yourself with the laws so that you do not commit any act considered criminal by the law of the country visited. Refrain from all trafficking in illicit drugs, arms, antiques, protected species and products or substances that are dangerous or prohibited by national regulations.

The advice above is based on the Global Code of Ethics for Tourism of the World Tourism Organization.

> *"Tourism has been identified by more than half of the world's poorest countries as an effective means to take part in the global economy and reduce poverty. "*
>
> United Nations WTO

Machu Picchu & Amazon River

Please help protect and conserve the environment

INDIGENOUS CULTURES

The Amazon River and its forests, is an expression of the explosion of life. Not only millions of species of plants and animals live in these rainforests, but also many Indians call the jungle "home".

In fact, on January 18, 2007, FUNAI reported that it had confirmed the presence of 67 different tribes "uncontacted" in Brazil. The term "uncontacted" refers to indigenous groups living in the Amazon jungle that do not have any contact with the outside world.

Today, nearly 70 indigenous groups still have no regular contact with modern civilization and stay away from any intruder. The Brazilian government's policy towards these groups is to leave them alone as they want to live. Therefore, not much is known about these groups, as they continue into the woods whenever the "whites" could be closer.

You should keep in mind that in Brazil, before any foreigner visits an Indian reservation, you must request permission from the National Indigenous Foundation (FUNAI), which is the Brazilian government body that establishes and carries out policies relating to Indians.

This institution is responsible for protecting the lands traditionally inhabited by these communities, besides being responsible for preventing invasions of indigenous lands by outsiders.

What is the FUNAI?

The FUNAI is composed of several departments, one of which is the General Coordination Unit of uncontacted Indians (CGII), which was established in 1987. It is dedicated to the protection of different indigenous groups that have very little contact, precisely so that they can remain virgins with their customs and way of life, thus avoiding any contamination they may receive from any outsider and simultaneously protecting their environment.

It is important to know that the department was founded as a result of death and disease caused by visitors and missionaries who previously sought to make contact with previously isolated tribes. Therefore, to avoid these unfortunate situations, the FUNAI will discuss and consider whether your application meets all the requirements. If it does, they will issue the respective permit for you to visit the reserve.

Why Indigenous Have Disappeared

Unfortunately, indigenous peoples have been disappearing along with the land they live on. This has happened since Europeans began to colonize their land

500 years ago. Unknowingly, the first European explorers brought diseases like smallpox, measles, influenza, and other more common diseases. Unfortunately, the Indians had no immunity against these diseases because they had never been exposed to them. Because of the interaction between the indigenous people and those outside their own circles, more than 90 percent of indigenous people died from diseases that we now regard as minor ones.

Besides disease as a major issue, for many years, indigenous groups have been expelled and killed by settlers who wanted their land. In other situations, the indigenous groups were enslaved in sugar plantations or mining operations. However, until some 40 years ago, the lack of roads kept many settlers from reaching deeper into indigenous territories, but this situation has been changing recently.

With the construction of more roads, mainly financed by logging and oil companies, ranchers and miners are coming into contact with the tribes. Together, these business conglomerates have opened up vast areas of the Amazon, which have made exploitation and destruction of millions of hectares of forest each year possible. Of course, it has irreparably damaged the habitat of many tribes.

Don't They Own The Rainforest?

The fact is that these indigenous peoples have inhabited the Amazon rainforest for thousands of years,

Machu Picchu & Amazon River

and this has been their home since then. They were born and died there, for many generations. In fact, the first accounts reported on these people are in the manuscripts made by European explorers, indicating that the Amazon peoples were a much denser population than today. Many of these original peoples, the Caribs, (named after the Caribbean), have completely disappeared, and many others have very few remnants remaining of their culture.

Sadly, although these indigenous peoples were the owners of these lands, living there for thousands of years, they have no "titles" of these lands. As a result, governments and other outsiders do not recognize their rights to land. The Indians are moved to different areas, sometimes very close to heavily populated cities, making them live in extreme poverty because they have no skills to live in the city.

For example, they may have more knowledge about medicinal plants and forest foods than any university scientist who has taken a lifetime studying in the subject. Nevertheless, when it comes to buying groceries at any store, these same Indians fail miserably. They do not know understand the value of the currency or goods since everything they need is taken from the forest.

Little by little, this process of extermination of indigenous people is not be as aggressive and brazen as it was when Europeans arrived, but it has continued in a more subtle way that can be even disguised with legality.

Another effective method of extermination is the provocation of war. When their land is invaded for dams, roads, or mine projects, the natives are always at a disadvantage since their weapons cannot compare to the modern and fatal weaponry of the settlers. Once the whites win the battle, trading companies force the indigenous people to labor in ruthless and inhumane conditions.

Previously, the Amazon rainforest was a giant shelter for the indigenous population, as there were no commercial reasons for colonists to enter the jungle. However, after the first half of last century, came the rubber boom. After that was the gold rush, and, today, colonists are after precious woods.

That is why, every day, we find less indigenous peoples, and those who survive are under pressure from new settlers. Some, like farmers, are considered by the government as legal settlers, but, to make matters worse, there are many illegal timber cutters, drug dealers, miners, and even biological traffickers trying to claim a share of the jungle, while their illicit business grows at the expense of the survival of indigenous peoples.

The Indigenous Groups Themselves

Anyway, today, there are still over 200 indigenous groups in the Amazon jungle, speaking 180 different languages and each has its own cultural heritage. If we only look at their languages, then we can reduce the languages to almost 30 in the Amazon rainforest. This shows us that, just like the flora and fauna and cultural diversity, the region is very rich.

Twenty-two different ethnic groups reside only in the northwest part of the Amazon rainforest in an area close to Brazil, Colombia and Venezuela. These 22 indigenous groups are different (Baniwa, Kuripako, Dow, Hupda, Nádob, Yuhupde, Bare, Warekena, Arapaso, Bara, Barasana Desana, Karapanã, Kube, Makuna, Miritytapuya, Pira-tapuya, Siriano, Tariana, Tucano, Tuyuca, Wanana, Tatu, Taiwan, Yurutí, Kakwa, and Nukak), and each speaks their own language. Although the languages are different, they all interact with each other in a large network of marriages, feasts, rituals, and commerce. The total population of these groups is about 65,000 people.

Another important group of uncontacted indigenous peoples is in the Upper Xingu, in the Brazilian state of Mato Grosso. There are 14 ethnic groups (Aweti, Kalapalo, Kamaiura Kuikuro, Matipu, Mehinako, Nahukuá, Trumai, Wauja, Yawalapiti, Ikpeng, Kaiabi his, and Yudja) in the area. The first 10 ethnic groups, such as the

Northwest Amazon, have different languages, but share the same rituals, have similar cultures, and they marry each other, participate at the same parties, and trade among themselves.

The last four groups are very different and have almost no contact with others, although there is still some cultural exchange.

There are other groups in the Amazon jungle. More than 70 groups have regular contact with outsiders, and, although the indigenous population is growing, they are still in great danger.

Therefore, and mainly in Brazil, access to remote areas where uncontacted tribes could be found is highly restricted, and we must remember that it is essential to observe these restrictions. These regulations help prevent unwanted interference and protect their communities from diseases to which they have little immunity.

Ayahuasca Be aware!

Similarly, other indigenous groups have opened their doors to travelers who want to learn about their culture. That has made the community tourism industry continue to grow in South America, but remember to take the ceremonies and rituals very seriously. Also, keep in mind that Ayahuasca and other psychoactive drugs play an important role in the religious life of some communities in the jungle, but it is illegal for foreigners to take these drugs.

Great Harm Done

Similarly, today the penetration into the forest by foreigners is doing great harm to indigenous traditions, habits, hunting and fishing, and their culture in general. Unfortunately, many tribes that have been decimated in confrontations with foreigners, and their vast knowledge regarding plants and animals have been lost forever.

As we have seen throughout our imaginary journey down the Amazon, some indigenous people live much the same as we do, and many others still live as their ancestors did thousands of years ago. These communities organize their daily lives differently than our culture. They obtain their food, medicine, and clothing mainly from the forest.

For example, most non-tribal children go to schools like ours. Indigenous children learn about the forest with their parents and others in their communities. They are taught how to survive in the woods. They learn to hunt and fish, and learn which plants are useful as drugs or food. Therefore, some of these kids know more about rainforests than scientists who have been studying the forest for many years.

Besides hunting, gathering wild fruits, nuts, and fish, the Indians also have small gardens and other food sources. They use sustainable farming methods called shifting cultivation where they first clear a small area of land and then burn it. Then they plant many types of plants to be used for food and medicine. After a few years, the soil has become too poor to harvest any crops, and the only thing that grows is weeds. Then they move on and start growing plants in a new area.

The original land is allowed to grow freely for another 10 or 15 years, before they grow again. Shifting cultivation is still practiced by indigenous groups that have access to large amounts of land.

However, with the growing number of foreign farmers that are new to the jungle and exploiters of the forest by other groups, indigenous people have been forced to remain in the same area. Obviously, the land becomes deserted after years of overuse and cannot be used for agriculture, with fatal results for these individuals.

As is well known, the natives worship the forest that has given them everything they needed while protecting them from foreigners. . They live what is called a sustainable existence, meaning they use of land without harming the plants and animals. As an Indian wise man once said, "The earth is our historian, our teacher, the provider of food, medicine, clothing, and protection. She is the mother of our race."

Machu Picchu & Amazon River

Are They Like Canaries in a Mine?

In the nineteenth century, lead miners took canaries in the mines with them because the birds were very sensitive to toxic gases. If the birds died, it was a warning to miners that they too would die, unless they fled the premises. Jason W. Clay has compared the rainforests and their inhabitants to the canary's miners. Today we can see that Indians are dying. However, we can no longer escape from the earth. We can only change our ways.

Within the next few decades, the fate of indigenous peoples is in our hands. They occupy fragile environments; they embody valuable knowledge that may well decide once and for all. A number of individuals, corporations, and some states are already implementing their own "final solution".

So the nineteenth century (and 20th and 21st) will be remembered either as the century where we destroyed much of the genetic and cultural diversity of the Earth or as the century in which people learned to live together and share knowledge in order to maintain diversity from which we all depend.

"Working together, we can make a world of difference."
    ----Rainforest Action Network

Thank You!

So my friend and colleagues, we finally have reached the end of the road.

I leave you with my best wishes for your next trip to the Amazon. I hope that this journey was a complete success and wish it transformed your life the way it has influenced mine.

Thank you for helping the people of the Amazon and taking care of our natural resources, but my most sincere thanks is for being such a great travel companion in this ship we call Planet Earth.

For more information about this book and the author, please visit:

www.AmazonRiverExpert.com

RESOURCES FOR YOUR AMAZON TRIP

Airports

Manaus
http://www.azworldairports.com/airports/a1210mao.cfm

Belem
http://www.aeropuertosdelmundo.com.ar/americadelsur/brasil/aeropuertos/belen.php

Iquitos
http://www.aeropuertosdelmundo.com.ar/americadelsur/peru/aeropuertos/iquitos.php

Leticia
http://www.aeropuertosdelmundo.com.ar/americadelsur/colombia/aeropuertos/leticia.php

Santarém
http://www.aeropuertosdelmundo.com.ar/americadelsur/brasil/aeropuertos/santarem.php

Airlines

Aero Republica Airlines
  http://www.aerorepublica.com/
  AEROPOSTAL *http://www.aeropostal.com/*
  AVENSA *http://www.avensa.com.ve*
  AVIOR *http://www.avior.com.ve*
  COPA Air *www.copaair.com*
  Lan Perú *http://www.lan.com/index-es-pe.html*
  LASER *http://www.aerolaser.com/*
  Lineas Aereas StarPeru
www.munimaynas.gob.pe/Turismo/IquitosMonumental.htm
  Lloyd Aero Boliviano *www.labairlines.com.bo*
  Rico Airlines
www.voerico.com.br/empresa/site/default_pers.asp
  RUTACA *http://www.rutaca.com*
  Satena Airlines *http://www.satena.com/*
  Taca Air *http://www.taca.com*
  TAM Airlines *http://www.tam.com.br/*
  Tames Airlines
  https://www4.tame.com.ec/eticketen/index.aspx
  Trip Airlines *http://www.voetrip.com.br/*
  VARIG Airlines
  http://portal.varig.com.br/ar/varig/index_html
  VOEGOL Airlines
  http://www.voegol.com.br/col/Paginas/Home.aspx

Machu Picchu & Amazon River

Buses

Cruz del Sur en Peru
http://www.cruzdelsur.com.pe/inicio_2.php

Ecuador Buses
http://www.getquitoecuador.com/quitotransport/quito_ecuador_bus_service.html

Eucatur
http://www.eucatur.com.br/historia.php

Expreso Los Llanos
http://www.expresosllanos.com/

Expreso Occidente
Prado de María, Caracas, Venezuela Teléfono: +58 212 632 2670/3132

Trans Esmeraldas
Terrestre Cumandá office # 53-54.Terminal Quito, Ecuador +593 2 2572 996

Boats

Boats to Iquitos
Transportes Eduardo Yurimaguas o Iquitos, Peru tel. +516 535 2991

Holland American
http://es.hollandamerica.com/enes/main/Main.action

Transporte Golphino
http://www.transportegolfinho.com/index-eng.html

Transtur
http://transturperu.vilabol.uol.com.br/transporte2.htm

More Interesting Places

Store Casa Brazil Uirapuru
Calle8, #10-35, Leticia. Teléfono: +579 8592 7056 Preguntar por Carlos

Floating House
http://www.amazonascolombia.com/indexama.php?pg=opt5&viewfoto=opt5|hot|4

Pucallpa City
http://www.pucallpa.com/

Yurimaguas City
http://www.enyurimaguas.com/

Monkey Island
http://www.amazonas.gov.co/index.cfm?doc=displaypage&sid=62&cid=26&pid=25

Leticia Serpertarium
http://www.nativa.org/webingles/amazoonas_project.html

Amacayacu Natinal Park
http://www.amazonas.gov.co/index.cfm?doc=displaypage&sid=62&cid=26&pid=26

Reserve Pacaya-Samiria
http://www.pacaya-samiria.com/frame_spa.htm

Reserve Palmari
http://www.palmari.org/vcd/en/inicio/index.htm

Machu Picchu & Amazon River

Aditional Resources

Peruvian Amazon
http://www.regionloreto.gob.pe/
City of Leticia, Colombia
http://www.leticia-Amazonas.gov.co/index.shtml
City of Tabatinga, Brazil
http://www.portaltabatinga.com.br/
Iquitos City
http://www.munimaynas.gob.pe/Turismo/IquitosMonumental.htm
Dra. Donna Schwontkowski
www.DrDonnaHerbalTraining.com
Ecoturismo Estratégico
http://www.ecoturismoestrategico.com/
Ecoviages en Santarém
http://ecoviagem.uol.com.br/brasil/para/santarem/agencia-turismo/agencia-jm/
Colombian Amazon
http://www.amazonas.gov.co/index.cfm
Exchange rate
http://www.xe.com/
Go2Peru
http://www.go2peru.com/lan_peru2.htm
Amazon Herbs
www.AmazonHerbalRemedies.com
Iniciativa Amazónica
www.iamazonica.org.br/home/index.php?id=conteudoESP.php

Mynor Schult
www.AmazonRiverExpert.com
Sustainable Travel
https://sustainabletravelinternational.org/documents/op_carboncalcs.html
Swimming the Amazon
http://www.amazonswim.com/main.php
Walking the Amazon
http://es.walkingtheamazon.com/

Videos that you must watch

Matamala Turtle
http://www.youtube.com/watch?v=5T2gU87t4KU
Anaconda
http://www.youtube.com/watch?v=2cRoeOp8h_I
Piranhas Fishing
http://www.youtube.com/watch?v=nsKhfvHDnS8
The Amazon River
http://www.youtube.com/watch?v=0q_zr2FESVU
Amazonas, Colombia
http://www.youtube.com/watch?v=vyBv6sT0NEw
Iquitos, Peru
http://www.youtube.com/watch?v=DwJufrQPQGE&feature=related
Ed Walking the Amazon
http://www.youtube.com/watch?v=kNlHe8KXsKs
Strel Swimming the Amazon
http://www.youtube.com/watch?v=ce432_JmdB8

Machu Picchu & Amazon River

To learn more and save hundreds of dollars on travel and experiential tours to the Amazon, please visit

www.AmazonRiverExpert.com

Please feel free to share your comments

with the author at:

mynor@AmazonRiverExpert.com

Notes

Machu Picchu & Amazon River

Notes

Printed in Great Britain
by Amazon